"In *Women Leading Well*, Emily Dean invites readers to seek out who God has made them to be so they can faithfully do what God has called them to do. Her down to earth writing makes this book accessible, and her biblical knowledge makes it even more practical and inspiring. Emily has certainly provided a much needed, relevant call to action for women in any season of life."

—**Missie Branch**, assistant dean to students
for women and director of graduate life,
Southeastern Baptist Theological Seminary

"Guiding women to consider that God has called and gifted them to lead in various capacities, Emily Dean offers biblical wisdom for those seeking to steward their influence well. *Women Leading Well* reminds me that leadership is chiefly about loving God, loving others, and abiding in Christ to accomplish the task."

—**Julia Higgins**, *Empowered and Equipped* and assistant professor of ministry to women, Southeastern Baptist Theological Seminary

"Emily has captured both the unique ways God calls women to influence others, whether you are in a ministry setting, the marketplace, or in your home. The pages of this book will provide the handles you need to move forward and will give you the scriptural basis to lead with boldness and dependence on the God who created you for this task."

—**Kelly King**, manager of devotional publishing and
women's ministry training, Lifeway Christian Resources

"In *Women Leading Well*, Emily Dean shares theological and practical insights that draw the reader in and help her understand what leadership is and how leadership plays a vital role in her life. I found this book to be straight forward, yet deep and meaningful. A beautiful and timely work for all women."

—**Andrea Lennon**, women's ministry specialist,
Arkansas Baptist State Convention

"Leadership knows no gender. The Lord Jesus calls and equips women for ministry leadership in his church. How, then, should they lead? Emily Dean answers that question skillfully, writing from a place of biblical wisdom and personal experience. I was instructed, humbled, encouraged, and equipped by *Women Leading Well*. A valuable go-to resource for leadership training, and one that I'll be using and recommending to others."

—**Eric Schumacher**, associate pastor, Grand
Avenue Baptist Church, Ames, Iowa

"Emily Dean brings out treasures both old and new in this work. *Women Leading Well* first unfolds the necessary doctrines of universal priesthood, ministerial calling, and spiritual gifts through careful theological exegesis of Scripture. But the most enlightening part of this fine guidebook appears with her wise practical advice. Our Lord's churches will thrive for God's glory as they learn to encourage their leadership."

—**Malcolm B. Yarnell III**, research professor of theology,
Southwestern Baptist Theological Seminary

WOMEN LEADING WELL

WOMEN LEADING WELL

Stewarding the Gift of Ministry Leadership

EMILY W. DEAN

Foreword by Katie McCoy

ACADEMIC
BRENTWOOD, TENNESSEE

To my husband, Jody:
You have encouraged me to live out my calling
at every step in our journey together.
We make a great team.

To my children, Lydia and James:
May you both steward well the leadership gifts
God has given you for his glory.

Contents

Foreword

When I told people I was a seminary student, I came to dread the question that inevitably followed: "What are you going to *do* with your degree?" I'd fumble about for a response that seemed to suffice, but the truth was, I didn't know. My biblical convictions guided my understanding of women in the church. But where did that leave me?

I was hardly alone. Each year, hundreds of women enroll in theological education without a clearly defined career track but undeterred in their zeal to contribute to kingdom ministry. Their posture for service is not dependent on their position in a church. And their spiritual foremothers reach back through centuries.

In the late 1600s, a young British woman pseudonymously published a lament and an appeal to the women of her generation. At twenty-eight, Mary Astell (1666–1731) dreamed of a community of women who dedicated their lives to developing their character and deepening their minds. Her work, *A Serious Proposal to the Ladies*, called on Christian women to fulfill all that it meant to be a disciple of Christ, to rid themselves of "unconcerning and unprofitable Matters," and to become all that God intended them to be.

Her motive had nothing to do with what women would *do*, but with who women would *be*—not a position in a church, but a posture of the heart. She had no desire to overstep Scripture, but simply to honor God: "Our only Contention shall be that [men] not out-do us in promoting his Glory who is Lord both of them and us."

Over 300 years later, we can still find among female followers of Christ the desire to serve, to leverage their gifts, aptitudes, and opportunities for the kingdom of God—and to lead others in that holy pursuit.

Women are natural communicators and influencers. We are hardwired for verbal expression and relational connection quite literally from the womb. We influence the emotions, actions, and decisions of others throughout our relationships. Yet, despite our role in shaping the future of those under our care, we sometimes have trouble seeing ourselves as leaders.

Perhaps it's because of our theological cultures, in which leadership is often conflated with the pastoral office. Perhaps it's because of our own experiences, from which we may carry the hurt of being mistreated or misunderstood. Or perhaps it's because we've not yet learned the wisdom of Mary Astell, who reminds us that we do not need a formal position of leadership to excel in the spiritual ministry of leadership.

Emily Dean has presented us with a manual of sorts. This manual enables every woman—regardless of situation, background, or temperament—to see herself as a leader, a "compelling force" of influence. This influence is entirely in harmony with—indeed, expressive of—her design as a woman created in God's image.

Weaving together biblically based wisdom on spiritual gifts, stewarding influence, godly ambition, and relational conflict, Emily guides her readers to inhabit their ministry of leadership with excellence. And she empowers them to embrace their responsibility to lead from a spiritual posture of service no matter what their ministry position.

May every woman who reads this work find the courage to ask not what she will do, but who she will be.

Katie McCoy

Acknowledgments

This book is written because of the countless women on whose shoulders I stand in ministry. My earliest memories of seeing women lead in ministry came from my family. My grandmother Mary Belle, whose legacy of sixty-plus years of faithful Bible teaching, along with leading and serving on various committees, and my grandmother Lula, who led in Bible teaching as well, formed a deep impression on me. My mother, Pam, has used her musical, administrative, and teaching gifts in a variety of capacities in the church. I am forever marked by their examples of faithful service.

Thank you to mentors and friends in ministry who have gone before me, encouraged me, and shown me the way to use my God-given gifts. I have learned so much from all the women God has brought into my life who have taught me what it means to lead well. Jane Wilson, especially, was the first woman I knew who had been to seminary and was serving in vocational ministry. Jane, I never questioned whether there would be a place for me in theological education because of your example.

Thanks to the team at B&H Academic for believing in this project. Your support from day one has encouraged me to press on. Audrey, Michael, Lindsay, and Renée, thank you for helping me navigate this process.

Thanks to the men in my family whose encouragement and support have helped me become the woman I am today. My grandfather Owen had a passion for all his grandchildren to have the opportunity to pursue higher education, which encouraged me to keep going and earn a PhD. My dad, Robert John, has always emboldened me to reach my full potential. My husband, Jody, has created spaces for me to grow and thrive in ministry as well. Thanks for your sacrificial leadership in our family.

Thanks to my children, Lydia and James, who have joined me in this process by praying for me and allowing me to share your stories. I am grateful for how you participate with your dad and me in ministry. You are a part of kingdom work.

And finally, it is because of God's grace in my life that I am able to share this book with you. Words fail to express my gratitude for how God can take my meager fishes and loaves and multiply them for his glory.

Introduction

W omen" and "leadership" are two words that when combined bring up a lot of feelings. Strong feelings. Should women be leaders? How should women be leaders? In what ways should women lead? And that's just in the broader culture, not to mention the church! So much confusion exists that it can be overwhelming for women desiring to serve in ministry.

As a woman who prepares women for ministry leadership, common questions I am often asked are, "Are there opportunities available to me as a woman?" and "How should I lead as a woman?" The short answer to the first question is yes! Women can and should use their gifts to lead. The long answer to these questions is the opportunities available to you depend on your context and theological heritage. Yet you will likely find yourself already leading in many ways when you better understand leadership. Rather than focusing on what women should not do in leadership, the emphasis should be on what women are doing to lead in a variety of ways.

Many leadership principles are universal, bearing no relationship to the gender of the leader. But what does it mean to lead with those principles as a woman? The purpose of this book is not to outline precisely which leadership titles a woman should hold. Instead, this resource focuses on examining leadership principles for women serving in ministry leadership so that they may better learn to capitalize on the unique strengths they have to offer as women.

While not exhaustive, as much can be said on this topic, the principles included are derived from biblical examples of women leading, as well as leadership research, personal ministry experience, and a compilation of countless conversations with women serving in ministry leadership. Included throughout are reflections from women leading in a variety of ministries. Finally, the book concludes with encouragement for male leaders who champion women leading well. Whether a seasoned leader or just beginning in ministry, may this book offer you encouragement in your journey as you steward the gift of ministry leadership.

PART ONE

Foundations for Leading Well

For we are his workmanship, created in
Christ Jesus for good works, which God
prepared ahead of time for us to do.

—EPHESIANS 2:10

Preparing for ministry leadership begins with understanding your leadership potential. Recognizing that you are a leader, called and gifted for service in the church, is essential to building a foundation for leading with excellence. Being aware of your influence upon others allows you to lead with purpose and perspective. In part 1, we will discover the basis for leadership, explore calling, and examine spiritual gifts for ministry.

1

You Are a Leader

A God-fearing woman named Lydia, a dealer in purple
cloth from the city of Thyatira, was listening. The
Lord opened her heart to respond to what Paul was
saying. After she and her household were baptized, she
urged us, "If you consider me a believer in the Lord,
come and stay at my house." And she persuaded us.

—ACTS 16:14–15

There she was, staring at me with those bright eyes full of
wonder yet also full of dependence. This little person who
recently burst into my life was looking back at me with a look of
total trust that I would care for her every need. Like many new
moms, I felt totally overwhelmed. Yet strangely enough, it was in
those moments of early motherhood that I came to see myself as a
leader. I had never really thought about all the leadership decisions

I would have to make daily and in rapid succession. In those days, which turned into weeks and months, my leadership skills strengthened. By the time our daughter was about six months old, I was running a smooth schedule at our house. I had become a leader to my child.

Women and Influence

Often, I hear women say, "I'm not a leader" or "I don't think I can lead anyone." Before having a baby, I did not think that motherhood would require leadership skills. I was surprised to find out that not only were leadership skills necessary, but on most days, they were required for survival! Now, please do not hear me say leadership and motherhood are synonymous for women. Women can and do lead in a multitude of ways with or without being a mother. My point in sharing my story is that sometimes we are already leading in ways we don't realize. Before having children, I served in ministry leadership, discipling young women for several years. Yet, motherhood opened my eyes to see the leadership skills God was developing in me. How about you? When did you first begin to see yourself as a leader?

At its core, leadership implies influence. Contrary to cultural beliefs, leadership involves far more than holding a position or title.[1] Wielding influence means that we have "the capacity or power of persons or things to be a *compelling force* on or produce effects on the actions, behavior, opinions, etc., of others" (emphasis

---

[1] Ken Blanchard, Phil Hodges, and Phyllis Hendry, *Lead Like Jesus Revisited: Lessons from the Greatest Leadership Role Model of All Time* (Nashville: Thomas Nelson, 2016), 4.

mine).[2] A compelling force? Think about whether you are a compelling force to influence the actions and behaviors of others. That should make us pause and think about what we say and how we act in front of others.

All of us influence someone. Whether it's one person or thousands of people, we impact the people we are around. If leadership is synonymous with influence, then we are all leaders. We lead people whether we realize it or not. Some of us are more reluctant leaders, such as Moses in Exodus 4: "God, send someone else!" Then some of us are bold leaders like Isaiah in Isaiah 6: "God, send me!" In whatever way you see yourself, God has a place and space for you to lead and influence others.

Women and Biblical Leadership

Women have a unique gift of influence. God has given women a remarkable ability to be a compelling force in the lives of those around them. As servants of the Lord, women are influential to other believers. As wives, women have a substantial impact on their husbands. As mothers, women are incredibly significant in the lives of their children. As employers and employees, women are influential in the workplace.

From the opening pages of Scripture, God reveals the value he has placed on women as image-bearers of God. In Gen 1:27 we see that God created human beings, male and female, equal in worth and value but distinct in design. In verse 28, God gave them both a privilege and a responsibility when he bestowed on them dominion over

---

[2] Dictionary.com, s.v. "influence," accessed August 29, 2022, https://www.dictionary.com/browse/influence?s=t.

the earth. Since the beginning, women have been given the opportunity to make an imprint on humanity, whether for good or evil.

Often, thoughts of female influence in the Bible go immediately to Eve, who, when tempted by the serpent, ate the fruit and offered it to her husband in Genesis 3. Yet God restored her, and just one chapter later, Eve made an influential statement of faith.[3] She proclaimed to her husband that she had received a child "with the LORD's help" (4:1). Failure did not have the last word in Eve's life. She returned to the Lord in faith, and God used her as the mother of all humanity.

Examples abound in Scripture of women who used their influence for good to the glory of God. In the Old Testament, Miriam, described as a prophetess, courageously looked out for her brother Moses and led women in worship after the exodus. Ruth boldly joined her mother-in-law to go to Israel when it would have been much easier to return to her homeland. Consider Deborah, who judged the Israelites with skillful discernment. Lesser known is Jael, who engaged in a surprise attack against the Canaanite commander Sisera. Jael was the main subject of the first devotion I wrote for publication. Little did I know I had been assigned to write about a female assassin! Yet she, along with other women such as Rahab, acted audaciously to save the Israelites. Esther is another example of a woman who called her people to pray and fast and then risked her own life to speak up on behalf of the Jews.[4] Despite the surmounting obstacles, these women boldly trusted God and stepped out in faith to protect others. God worked through them to preserve his people.

---

[3] Elyse Fitzpatrick and Eric Schumacher, *Worthy: Celebrating the Value of Women* (Bloomington, MN: Bethany House, 2020), 66.

[4] Exodus 2; 15; Josh 2; Judg 4; Ruth 1:16–17; 2:2; Esth 4:16; 7:3–4.

In the New Testament we see the example of Anna, another prophetess, who proclaimed the truth of God's redemption. Mary Magdalene, Mary, and Martha served Jesus faithfully and valiantly proclaimed Jesus as Lord. Dorcas was a servant leader among women in the early church, while Priscilla taught the way of God alongside her husband, Aquila. Priscilla and her husband even risked their lives for Paul. Phoebe, a deaconess, likely delivered the letter from Paul to the Romans at great personal risk.[5] Then there's Lydia, who made sure all her household came to faith in Christ.[6] These are just a few of the women mentioned in the New Testament who used their influence to point others to the one true God. Let's take a closer look at the life of one of these women to see how Lydia used her influence to lead others.

The Leadership of Lydia

Lydia was a woman who led faithfully in her circumstances. Scripture doesn't indicate that she sought leadership opportunities, but she was a faithful leader as circumstances arose. Here are a few principles we can observe from her life.

Lydia Led through Humility

By all accounts in the ancient world, Lydia was an accomplished woman. She was a business owner and, being a seller of purple

---

[5] Robert H. Mounce, *Romans*, The New American Commentary 27 (Nashville: B&H, 1995), 272–73, Logos.

[6] Luke 2:36–38; John 11:27; 12:3; 20:18; Acts 9:36–42; 16:11–15; 18:24–26; Rom 16:1–3.

cloth, was likely quite wealthy.[7] We know that she had enough living accommodations to have a household and offer Paul and his companions a place to stay. Lydia could have taken pride in all her accomplishments and thought she did not need God. She could have considered herself a "self-made woman." Yet Scripture tells us she was a worshipper of God. We do not know whether she was a Jewish convert, but we do know she had a tender heart for God.[8] God opened her heart to listen to Paul, and she humbled herself to respond to the message of truth.

Lydia Led through Confidence and Integrity

Lydia took the initiative to make sure her entire household heard the good news of Jesus. Then she boldly urged Paul to stay with them longer so that they could listen to more teaching. Lydia had a lot at stake with her newfound faith. As a businesswoman, her reputation was on the line, but she chose to identify herself and her household with Jesus Christ. Lydia demonstrated courage by choosing to follow Jesus regardless of the cost to her business or reputation. Lydia took opportunities to lead with confidence and integrity.

Lydia Led through Professionalism

We know Lydia was a business owner. She was a purple cloth dealer, which meant she likely ran a lucrative business catering to

---

[7] Mike Mitchell, "Lydia," in *Holman Illustrated Bible Dictionary*, ed. Chad Brand et al., (Nashville: Holman Bible, 2003), 1060, Logos.

[8] Mitchell, 1060, Logos.

royalty.[9] Any woman running her own business knows that leadership takes organization. You must manage inventory, sales, and customers—just to name a few. The expectations for excellence in service are high, and competence is essential. To remain in business, professionalism would have been a necessary component of Lydia's leadership.

Lydia Led through Showing Concern for Others

We know Lydia and the members of her household were baptized, so she did not stop with herself when she became saved. She made sure her family met Jesus too. Not only did Lydia likely organize goods and services, but she also organized people. When she became a Christian, she sent word to her household. She led through creating a space for her people to hear about God and became an active leader in the church that developed.[10]

Lydia Led through Practical Wisdom

At the very end of Acts 16:15, we see a crucial piece of information concerning Lydia's influence. Scripture says she persuaded Paul to stay with her and her household. Lydia displayed wisdom, using her gift of influence for those in her household to be introduced to Jesus. Scripture doesn't say she nagged. It doesn't say she coerced. It does say she strongly urged Paul to

---

9 John B. Polhill, *Acts*, The New American Commentary 26 (Nashville: Broadman & Holman, 1992), 349.

10 Polhill, 349.

stay.[11] She didn't back down. She didn't give up. She wisely used her persuasion skills to give them more time to hear about the gospel. Lydia was a *compelling force* in spreading the gospel to the European church.

Women and the Church

When it comes to discussions on women leading in the church, the conversation generally centers on biblically appropriate roles. What can and should women do in the church? Understanding the Bible as one complete narrative from Genesis to Revelation gives us insight into the value of women in church leadership. The Bible provides many examples of women leading in a variety of ways. While some might say these examples go outside the norm of cultural mores at that time, that God would choose to include these examples in the canon of Scripture highlights their importance even more. Biblical examples of women leading reveal that women can and should lead in some ways. The extent to which women participate in leadership depends upon each church's theological tradition, which is where it often gets confusing and complex because churches may vary in belief and practice. On either end of the spectrum, views on the subject range from women can lead nothing in the church to women can lead anything, with many churches finding themselves somewhere between.

The struggle in these conversations often lies in understanding key passages regarding women in Scripture, primarily 1 Cor 11:3–16; 14:33–36; and 1 Tim 2:9–15. At first glance, it can

---

[11] Strong's Greek #3849, "Persuade," https://ref.ly/logosref/Greek Strongs.3849, Logos.

seem as though Paul was advocating that women do nothing in the church. Yet how could he say that women "should remain silent" in 1 Corinthians 14 when he gave instructions for women praying and prophesying three chapters earlier? Author Ken Hemphill clarifies in *You Are Gifted*:

> We can, however, conclude that Paul is not teaching that a woman should not participate in discussion that has the goal of Christian instruction, nor is he banning her from ever speaking in the assembly. Paul would not contradict his earlier teaching that was inspired by the Spirit. We must then conclude that Paul allowed women to pray and prophesy when done with the right spirit and according to the tradition of the churches.[12]

In all these passages, Paul called attention to orderly worship as he reminded the Corinthians that "God is not a God of disorder but of peace" (1 Cor 14:33). The focus of his conversation was giving instructional guidance on how to conduct worship systematically.[13] Keeping in mind the context of these discussions allows us to more fully understand Paul's instructions.

That women were invited to learn at all in worship marked a stark contrast to Judaism. Lea and Griffin observe:

> Paul's command that the women "learn" reflects Christian practice which differed from the customs of Judaism. Judaism would enforce physical silence on women without

---

[12] Ken Hemphill, *You Are Gifted: Your Spiritual Gifts and the Kingdom of God* (Nashville: B&H, 2009), 114.

[13] Mark Taylor, *1 Corinthians*, ed. E. Ray Clendenen, The New American Commentary 28 (Nashville: B&H, 2014), 363.

concern for their growth in knowledge. At this point Paul was not borrowing from his Jewish heritage but was reflecting as a Christian a greater appreciation for the role of women in spreading the gospel.[14]

If order was the focus of Paul's teaching, there had to be a reason for him to be concerned about disorder. Some scholars have contended that women were causing confusion by interrupting and usurping authority in the services, particularly in the church in Ephesus.[15] In the church at Corinth, some believe women were trying to outdo or embarrass their husbands by questioning their prophecies in public.[16] Whatever was happening, something was creating disorder that compelled Paul to give these churches instructions on orderly worship.

When discussing these passages with women in ministry leadership classes, American students generally state that they do not wear head coverings when attending worship services in the United States—unless hats are fashionable in their culture. They also say they do not avoid gold and pearls at church. Growing up in the South in the '80s and '90s, I saw pearls everywhere at church on Easter Sunday! Functionally, in many US churches, depending on denomination, we assume those parts of the passages to be cultural applications specific to the churches to whom the Pauline letters were originally written. Thus, the question becomes, what is the timeless principle in these passages? To whatever extent you understand these

---

[14] Thomas D. Lea and Hayne P. Griffin, *1, 2 Timothy, Titus*, The New American Commentary 34 (Nashville: Broadman & Holman, 1992), 98.

[15] Lea and Griffin, 97.

[16] Richard L. Pratt Jr., *I & II Corinthians*, Holman New Testament Commentary 7 (Nashville: Broadman & Holman, 2000), 250.

passages, it is critical to keep in mind the whole context of Scripture and distinguish the principle from the cultural application. Think about the women we've discussed and the leadership roles they played in the Bible. We must be careful not to isolate passages but rather to look at them considering the whole counsel of God's Word. Scripture is clear that women are vital to the kingdom of God!

To help women determine where to use their gifts, churches can clearly define their congregation's beliefs about women leading. If women know the standard, then they will be more confident in leading where they are encouraged to do so.[17] If your church does not have a clear outline for where women can fill leadership roles, talk to your church leadership and ask if that could be outlined.

Much of the challenge in understanding leadership roles for women in the church comes from the differences in the twenty-first-century church versus the early church. The early church did not have multiple staff positions like many modern churches. The pastor/elder structure was much less complex in the early church. In the last twenty years, the number of megachurches in the US (2,000 or more weekly attendees[18]) has more than doubled, which naturally increases the staff structure.

Yet while megachurches exist, in denominations such as the Southern Baptist Convention (SBC), most churches still have memberships of 250 or fewer.[19] Bi-vocational ministry is common

---

[17] Kadi Cole, *Developing Female Leaders: Navigate the Mindfields and Release the Potential of Women in Your Church* (Nashville: Thomas Nelson, 2019), 18.

[18] Warren Bird, "Megachurch Books?," Leadership Network, May 17, 2012, https://leadnet.org/megachurch/.

[19] "The Changing Face of Small Churches," *Vision Magazine* 70, no. 2 (Fall 2014): 8, https://issuu.com/neworleansseminary/docs/visionfall2014_online?e=5726383/10939947.

among both men and women in many churches. If we only look to the large church staff structure, we may miss opportunities for ministry leadership right in front of us.

My experiences serving in ministry leadership have been overwhelmingly positive. God has continued to give me ministry opportunities, whether informal or formal, wherever he has led me to serve. My husband and family have been incredibly supportive, and I have been blessed to be encouraged by men and women with whom I serve. Their support has been crucial to my leadership growth.

Yet I have met enough women to know that experiences vary for women serving in ministry. If you have not received encouragement in leading, please know you are valuable to the church and the kingdom of God. Your gifts are needed for the church to grow and thrive. Author Carolyn Custis James rightly observes, "When half the church holds back—whether by choice or because we have no choice—everybody loses and our mission suffers setbacks."[20] So, instead of concentrating our discussions on how women should not lead in the church, let's focus on how women can and should lead. You are a leader!

Questions to Ponder

1. Do you view yourself as a leader? Why or why not?
2. In what ways do you influence others in your family, at work, or at church?

---

[20] Carolyn Custis James, *Half the Church: Recapturing God's Global Vision for Women* (Grand Rapids: Zondervan, 2011), 19.

3. In what ways do you believe it is biblically appropriate for women to lead in the church?

4. Our understanding of how women can and should lead also comes from our experiences. How have you seen women lead in the church? How has that shaped your perception of women in ministry leadership?

2

You Are Called

"Go, therefore, and make disciples of all nations,
baptizing them in the name of the Father and of the
Son and of the Holy Spirit, teaching them to observe
everything I have commanded you. And remember,
I am with you always, to the end of the age."

—MATTHEW 28:19–20

What am I called to do? I hear some variation of this question from women frequently. Usually, the follow-up question goes something like this: *What can I do as a woman in ministry?* The word *calling* gets thrown around a lot in Christian circles, but what does it mean to be called by the Lord Jesus? As women, is our calling any different than that of men? High school and college students (well, let's be honest, older adults too) wrestle with this idea of discovering what they are called to do. Often when people discuss their calling, they are talking about specific plans for their lives (e.g., *What job will I have?*). We tend to equate calling with career. Calling is a much broader topic. Sure, a specific calling can involve your occupation. However, our calling as believers goes far beyond what gives us a paycheck. Let's look at some basic ideas of what it means to be called by God.

What Does "Called by God" Mean?

Jesus Calls You to Himself

Before we can even begin to understand what we are supposed to do with our lives, we first need to know who is calling us. God created humans to be in relationship with him. Because that relationship was broken by the fall of man, we needed a way to restore our relationship with God (Genesis 3). God provided a way for humanity to be redeemed through Jesus's death and resurrection (Rom 5:6–8). Through Jesus, we can be restored to a right relationship with God.

So, what do we do? We respond. God initiates the relationship with us. We choose whether to respond in faith. Our calling is to have a relationship with God through Jesus Christ. When you become a believer, Jesus beckons you to himself (John 10:3). Your focus then is to know him (Isa 26:8). Arguably one of the New Testament's busiest defenders of the faith, the apostle Paul, still said his primary purpose was to know Christ (Phil 3:8). We can get so caught up in what we are supposed to do that we easily forget who we are supposed to know. More than anything you do for God, who you are as God's child matters most (John 1:12).

God created you for a relationship with him. Forgetting this concept is easy when you become busy serving Christ. There is always so much to do, and many needs must be met. Not only do we forget that God created us to be in a relationship with him, but also, we fail to remember this simple truth: God loves me. When ministry is demanding, we can quickly slip into thinking our value to God rests in what we do for him. Yet God loves you because he created you, not because of how much you can do for him. Jesus even reminded his disciples that ministry needs will always be there. Making time for a relationship with him was the most important thing they could do (Matt 26:11). Shouldn't it be most important for us too?

Jesus Calls You to Give Him Glory

We often hear the phrase "give God the glory." As a kid I remember learning a song that included the lyrics "Rise and shine, and give God the glory, glory."[1] It had a catchy tune, but I had no idea what it meant, other than I thought it must be something good given that we were singing it in church. God's glory is described as an attribute of God and a manifestation of his presence. The original Hebrew word, *kabod*, carries the concept of weightiness or gravity. In the sense of humans, glory means giving one honor achieved or the worth and esteem that goes with an inherited position.[2] Giving

---

[1] "Rise and Shine," Hymnary.org, https://hymnary.org/text/the_lord _said_to_noah_theres_gonna_be_a_.

[2] Eugene Carpenter and Philip Comfort, *Holman Treasury of Key Bible Words* (Nashville: B&H, 2000), 72, Logos.

God glory means we offer him the dignity and respect he deserves as Creator of the universe. We acknowledge the splendor of his majesty (Ps 96:9).

Why is it important to give God glory? First, God deserves our respect. He is the sovereign Lord of the universe. He is the Creator. We are his creation (Ps 95:6–7). Second, giving God glory gives our hearts delight (v. 1). Third, recognizing who God is helps us remember who we are. We remember "we are but dust" (103:14). We remember God is the only one who can fill our souls with joy. We recognize he can take care of what concerns us. We remember he is worthy of our praise.

How do we give him glory? We give God glory by representing him well in all we do (1 Cor 10:31). When we acknowledge God as our provider, when we treat people as we would want to be treated, or when we depend on him for strength in our weakness, we recognize the weightiness or gravity of who God is. Each time we acknowledge something God has done or who he is, we give him glory.

Jesus Calls You to Follow Him

That Jesus wants you to follow him may seem obvious since you are reading a book on ministry leadership. Likely you feel you have given your life to following Jesus. Yet I would like you to consider what that looks like in your life daily. Are you following the leading of the Holy Spirit throughout your day? Are you listening to the Lord as he speaks to you during the day, or is your communication with him limited to the moments you can sneak into your already busy schedule to read your Bible? Paul exhorted the Galatians to "walk by the Spirit" (Gal 5:16). Are you living a Spirit-led life, and what does that even mean?

When Jesus called his disciples, he simply said to them, "Follow me . . . and I will make you fish for people" (Matt 4:19). Jesus invited the disciples to be in relationship with him, learn from him, follow his ways, and teach others to do the same. The apostle Paul exhorted the Corinthians to follow his example as he followed the example of Christ (1 Cor 11:1). Living a Spirit-led life means we are actively seeking to grow in our relationship to Christ, listening to him, learning to follow his ways, and teaching others to do the same. Listening to the Lord, allowing him to lead you, and then following his direction is essential to being a disciple of Christ. Here are some checkpoints to determine whether you are allowing God to speak into your life regularly.

Are You Studying God's Word Daily?

Most of us would not think of going a day without food unless we are fasting. Food is essential to human life. Yet if God's Word is our daily bread (Matt 4:4), then shouldn't we treat it as essential? You may be thinking that some days you do not get anything out of God's Word. Think of it like this: There are days you eat food just for the sake of eating food. I have packed many peanut butter and jelly sandwiches for lunch in my lifetime. While not a gourmet delicacy, it sustains me when I need food. Then, some days, I get to eat my favorite foods, and I savor every bite. Often God gives you what you need to sustain you when reading the Bible. Then there will be days when the Word comes alive, and you feel as if God has just given you a gourmet meal. You need both, and you never know how God will choose to speak to you through his Word. If you don't read it, you will fail to receive the sustenance you need.

Are You Spending Time in Prayer?

Dozens of books have been written on prayer, but daily conversation with God is crucial to being led by God. I usually try to get my mornings started with a conversation with God and then continue that conversation throughout the day. When difficult conversations or decisions come, I am continually conversing with the Father, asking for his help, guidance, and wisdom. These prayers are often called breath prayers. Breath prayers are simply a sentence or two that you say to God, generally silently. For example, as someone is sharing a difficult situation with you, you may silently say to God, "Please give me wisdom in this moment." Seeing how God directs my thoughts in those moments when I am talking to him has been amazing. I must admit, though, that sometimes I lose focus and forget to pick back up the conversation. I can always tell when I have failed to pray throughout the day. Mishaps and missteps often characterize those days. But when I do listen to him, I am always in awe of how he guides me.

Are You Listening to Godly People in Your Life?

God often speaks through his people. While our first priority is to listen to God, sometimes God works through discussions with spiritually mature people. He speaks through pastors, teachers, counselors, mentors, friends, and family. The critical qualifier here is that you are surrounding yourself with people who are actively seeking to follow Jesus and that you listen to him yourself. While God can speak through anyone, he most often speaks through those listening to him. If you don't have these kinds of people in your life, pray and ask God to bring spiritually mature guides into your life. Then look for opportunities through your local church to get to know people who are faithfully following Jesus.

Are You Listening to the Circumstances in Your Life?

God determines the circumstances in which he places us (Job 14:5). He chose for you to be born in a particular place on a specific day. He chose your gender, ethnicity, hair color, eye color, and everything else about you (Ps 139:13–14). Even though we are told that we can be anything and do anything in American culture, the truth is we all have limitations. Time, resources, life circumstances, etc., all place natural limitations on our lives. Yet we can be and do anything God wants us to be and do. God generally works through the circumstances in which he has placed us. While our stories are continually being written, usually our stories can point us toward God's plan for our lives. Examine your life up to this point and see what God has already been doing. That may be an indicator of what direction he will take you next.

Jesus Calls You to Make Disciples

The primary assignment of a Christian believer is to make disciples. Jesus gave us this job description in Matt 28:19–20, the passage referred to as the Great Commission. Far too often, we lose this focus trying to build our own kingdoms or ministries. Our purpose for ourselves is not what matters. God's purpose for us gives us meaning and direction for life. We may have to return to this call repeatedly. If it seems too basic and you feel like you need to move on to higher things, then maybe you have lost sight of what matters to Jesus. Making disciples should be at the heart of everything you do as a Christian.

The call to make disciples is not gender specific. God instructs all believers, male and female, to make disciples. As noted in *Worthy*, "A Christian woman's vocation is simple: make disciples and teach them the truth about the One who has come."[3] Whom are you teaching? If you don't know whom you should disciple, then look around.

- Are there kids in your home?
- Are there family members seeking God?
- Are people in your workplace asking questions?
- Are there new believers in your church?

Opportunities are usually all around us if we begin to look. If we are not actively seeking to make disciples, we miss out on the main job God wants us to fulfill.

What about discipling other women? Sometimes I hear statements from women leaders such as, "I don't like ministering to other women because women can be so petty or difficult." While that may be an overgeneralization in my opinion, even if the statement were true, that demonstrates an even greater need to disciple women. Titus 2 gives us a clear vision for older women discipling younger women. With women comprising more than half of the membership in most evangelical Protestant churches, many women needing

---

[3] Fitzpatrick and Schumacher, *Worthy*, 192 (see chap. 1, n. 3).

discipleship can be found in the church.[4] The harvest is plentiful (Luke 10:2). Imagine what would happen if every woman in the church was discipled. Then those women would reach other women to disciple them. Our churches would be full of growing believers!

The idea behind discipleship is that we are disciples who make disciples who make disciples. Not only are we charged with making disciples, but also, we are commissioned to teach those we disciple how to replicate themselves. Replication shouldn't stop with those whom we are discipling. Ideally, the cycle will continue spreading the Word of God with each new disciple. My encouragement to you would be to keep an open mind about the people God wants you to disciple. Be careful to avoid ignoring or discounting individuals because you think they would be challenging to engage in discipleship. You never know whom God has in mind for you to invest your life.

Discerning a Specific Call

Up to this point, we have discussed God's general call to all believers, but what if you feel God is calling you to something specific? God does call certain people to certain tasks. We see evidence of God leading men and women to accomplish his purposes throughout Scripture. A particular call may be to a specific vocation or ministry. Both men and women can receive a specific call to ministry. A call to ministry is not more important than a calling to other vocations; however, it is a particular call God gives to certain

---

[4] "Religious Landscape Study: Gender Composition," Pew Research Center, accessed August 29, 2022, https://www.pewresearch.org/religion/religious-landscape-study/gender-composition/.

individuals. How do you know if that's where God is leading you, and what are your first steps?

As a college student, I began to sense God had something specific in mind for me. I had no idea what that might be. At event after event with the college ministry I attended, students, both men and women, would come forward saying they felt called to ministry. I was never one of those students. Maybe I was afraid it would become all too real if I said out loud what I sensed God was doing in my life. What if I was wrong? What if I completely misheard God's voice, or what if it was not God's voice at all? For those reasons I kept my thoughts to myself. However, the impression on my soul that God was calling me to ministry would not go away. It became stronger and stronger. I began to realize that God was calling me to vocational ministry.

What does vocational ministry mean? It means ministry is not only something you do as all believers are called toward, but it is also your vocation. According to Dictionary.com, "vocation" can be understood as "a particular occupation, business, or profession; *calling; a divine call to God's service or to the Christian life*"[5] (emphasis mine). Amazingly, even on a secular website, two of the four definitions of vocation involve service to God! So, your vocation is the main focus of what you do. Another way of looking at vocational ministry is that it is "understood as God setting someone apart to serve him, for the good of his people, by delivering the Word of God (in some way) to them."[6]

---

[5] Dictionary.com, s.v. "vocation," accessed June 20, 2022, https://www.dictionary.com/browse/vocation.

[6] Kristen Padilla, *Now That I'm Called: A Guide for Women Discerning a Call to Ministry* (Grand Rapids: Zondervan, 2018), 13.

Ministry as a vocation means it is the center of your life's work. Here are a couple of things to keep in mind about a call to ministry leadership:

God's Call to Ministry May or May Not Provide Your Income

With more women earning undergraduate degrees than men and more women entering the workforce than ever before, a natural question for women is "What will I do for income?"[7] Ministry leadership may include a full-time staff position at a church or ministry, but it may not. It may be something you desire to happen, and it may not. You may be firmly established in your career or educating your children at home but feel led to serve as a volunteer leader at your church. Then you may desire to serve full-time or part-time and receive your income from the ministry work that you do rather than other employment. I have served in ministry both ways. I have served as a volunteer leader while working at other employment or staying at home with children, and I have served in paid positions. The Lord's plan for me has continued to unfold one step at a time. He has provided what I have needed to serve him faithfully at each point. What has been most crucial in my journey is that I continue to follow Jesus and listen to the leading of the Holy Spirit.

One thing to consider is that often both men and women serve bi-vocationally. For many churches, that means they only have one

---

[7] Richard Fry, "U.S. Women Near Milestone in the College-Educated Labor Force," Pew Research Center, June 20, 2019, https://www.pew research.org/fact-tank/2019/06/20/u-s-women-near-milestone-in-the -college-educated-labor-force/.

full-time or part-time staff member, the senior pastor. Therefore, many ministry opportunities are going to be volunteer. Practically, this is often a budget issue more than a theological issue. That's not to say, though, if you have a sound rationale for your volunteer leadership to be a part-time or full-time staff position, that you should avoid asking. If you desire to leave your current employment to serve full-time in ministry, take it to the Lord. Ask him to open doors to give more of your time and attention to serving him.

God's Call to Ministry Will Continue to Pursue You

Generally, a desire to serve in ministry will be something that continues to come up in your life. The prophet Jeremiah said that even if he tried to quit speaking about the Lord, God's message would burn in his heart until he had to share it (Jer 20:9). He could not get away from God's call on his life, no matter how much he tried. If God continues to place a specific direction or desire on your heart, it would be a good idea to pay attention. God's purposes are persistent. In *A Life of Listening*, Leighton Ford encourages those pursuing God's call to *observe, reflect,* and *act.*

1. **Observe** what piques your interest or where God has led you up to this point.

2. **Reflect** by taking the steps listed in the chapter to read the Bible, pray, talk to spiritually mature advisers, and observe the circumstances of your life.

3. **Act** by doing the next right thing. Take whatever small steps you can to move in the direction God is leading you.[8]

---

[8] Leighton Ford, *A Life of Listening* (Downers Grove, IL: InterVarsity, 2019), 179–82.

Keep in mind this is God's call, not yours. If he chooses to call you, he has a plan for you to serve. He has gifted you to serve him, and he will show you where and how as you follow him.

Questions to Ponder

1. Have you ever struggled with what God is calling you to do? What is your perception of calling after reading this chapter?
2. What does wholehearted devotion to Jesus look like in your life?
3. How are you making disciples in your current context?
4. How are you allowing the Holy Spirit to lead you daily?

3

_____

You Are Gifted

A manifestation of the Spirit is given to each person for
the common good. . . . One and the same Spirit is active
in all these, distributing to each person as he wills.

—1 CORINTHIANS 12:7, 11

These days, we hear a lot about personality tests, though their
popularity comes and goes. When I was in college, I found
out which animal I am most like based on my personality. Then
I learned which letter of the alphabet most fits me. Now I have
learned that I am a number based on where I fall in the Enneagram.
A new test becomes all the rage with each generation. Personality
tests may be considered trendy, but let's not forget Scripture speaks
of unique giftings that are even greater. God gives spiritual gifts
to Christians to use as we minister to others. Often they coincide
with our personalities, but they are far more than a designation of

our makeup. Spiritual gifts are a manifestation of the Spirit of God. They reveal to us how God is working in and through us. What could be more amazing than that?

Discerning your spiritual gifts is a process. Just as there are no two people exactly alike, the manifestation of the Spirit through spiritual gifts will look a little different in each person. In this chapter, we will examine the why and what of spiritual gifts found in Scripture as well as how to discern and use the spiritual gifts God gives to us.

Why God Gives Spiritual Gifts

Spiritual Gifts Are for the Body of Christ

Spiritual gifts are given to us to build up the body of Christ. If God gives us a spiritual gift, he expects us to develop that gift for serving others. They are not provided to us so others can look at us and marvel at how awesome we are. God gives us spiritual gifts for the Holy Spirit to be demonstrated through us. It's all about how we are pointing people to Jesus Christ and helping them grow in Christlikeness. Because spiritual gifts are not for us, we should avoid holding them back for ourselves. Instead, we should use them and let God shine his light through us (Matt 5:16).

God Gives Spiritual Gifts as He Sees Fit

God gives us spiritual gifts because he desires to do so, and he chooses what spiritual gifts we get. Scripture says we can pray for gifts (1 Cor 14:1), but the Giver selects gifts. It is not up to us to choose which spiritual gift we want. It is up to God to decide which spiritual gift(s) he wants to give us. Knowing God gives spiritual gifts also frees us from passing judgment on which gift he may choose to give someone else. In leadership we should help others discover and develop their gifts, but it is not up to us to determine what gift God has chosen to bestow upon someone else. Our responsibility is to take the time to examine and develop what gifts God has allotted to us so that we may steward them well.

One Spirit Gives Spiritual Gifts

Spiritual gifts should bring unity of the Spirit. They should not bring division. If they are creating disharmony, you are likely using them for the wrong purpose. Everything about a spiritual gift should bring believers together and point people toward unity in Christ. Spiritual gifts are given to serve as a witness to the world of this great God whom we serve. As we help women discover and develop their gifts, we will empower them to build up the kingdom of God.

What Are Spiritual Gifts?

One understanding of spiritual gifts is that they are "individualized expressions of God's grace given us for the edification of the body."[1] Spiritual gifts demonstrate the Holy Spirit at work in and through us. God uses the spiritual gifts he gives us to accomplish his purposes on earth. Our job is to be available and willing to let God reveal his power through us. While variations exist among listings and definitions of gifts, the primary passages that focus on spiritual gifts are Rom 12:6–8; 1 Cor 12:8–10, 28–30; Eph 4:11; 1 Pet 4:7–11.

---

[1] Hemphill, *You Are Gifted*, 132 (see chap. 1, n. 12).

In Romans 12, Paul listed prophecy, service, teaching, exhorting, giving, leading, and showing mercy as gifts given to us by God's grace to serve in our unique parts of the body of Christ. These grace gifts motivate us to serve in the body of Christ. Think about what drives you. What do you most desire to do for Jesus at the very core of your being? Answering this question can be a good indicator of your grace gifts.[2]

The passage in Ephesians 4 lists apostles, prophets, evangelists, pastors/shepherds, and teachers as roles of gifting within the church. While some may consider this passage to be defining offices in the church, the passage's context discusses spiritual gifts given by God's grace. In urging unity of the Spirit, Paul noted, "Grace was given to each one of us according to the measure of Christ's gift" (v. 7). So, before listing these gifts, he said we *each* had received God's grace. He did not delimit anyone when he outlined the gifts listed in this passage. The roles define the essence of a person serving in the church rather than a specific office or paid staff position.

In 1 Corinthians 12–14, again Paul urged the Corinthian church to come together in unity of the Spirit. He showed them how they could work together to bring glory to God based on their giftings. In this passage, Paul listed wisdom, knowledge, faith, healing, miracles, prophecy, discernment, tongues, and administration as gifts of the Spirit. Paul explained in 12:7 that these gifts are a "manifestation of the Spirit . . . for the common good." When we use the spiritual gifts God gives us, the Holy Spirit reveals himself through us.

---

[2] Christi Gibson, *Given for Good: What's the Word on Spiritual Gifts* (Christi Gibson, self-published for the local church, 2014), 4.

The passage in 1 Peter 4 is shorter but reveals two distinct gifts to consider. First, Peter said, "If anyone speaks, let it be as one who speaks God's words; if anyone serves, let it be from the strength God provides" (v. 11). Speaking in this sense can refer to a broad category of gifts including apostleship, teaching, prophecy, tongues, and exhortation. In contrast, the serving gifts would include leadership, giving, helps, mercy, healing, and miracles.[3] Though equally important, leading behind the scenes often characterizes women utilizing serving gifts, while women with speaking gifts tend to lead in a more visible setting. Much discussion centers on the prominence of women utilizing speaking gifts, so let's more closely examine our understanding of speaking.

Speaking or teaching has often been preferred in many evangelical Christian contexts when referring to a woman giving a proclamation message. In this view, preaching is generally connected with the Sunday morning worship service in which a pastor regularly expounds on the Word of God. Surprisingly, neither Paul nor Peter included preaching as a spiritual gift. In discussing this gift of speaking, Peter did not use the most common words in the New Testament for preaching, *euaggelizo* and *kerysso*. Instead, he chose the word *laleo*, a broad term used to describe someone speaking, talking, preaching, proclaiming, teaching, or announcing.[4]

---

[3] Thomas R. Schreiner, *1, 2 Peter, Jude*, The New American Commentary 37 (Nashville: Broadman & Holman, 2003), 215.

[4] James Strong, *The Strongest Strong's Exhaustive Concordance of the Bible* (Grand Rapids: Zondervan, 2001), 1511.

The Greek *euaggelizo* refers to someone announcing good news,[5] while *kerysso* means proclaiming, crying out loud, declaring, and announcing.[6]

On the other hand, teaching is included in Scripture as a spiritual gift. It can be defined as "instructing members in the truths and doctrines of God's Word for the purposes of building up, unifying, and maturing the body."[7] The most frequent term used for teaching in the New Testament is *didasko*, a broad term meaning "to teach."[8] The word conveys the idea of telling someone what to do, providing instruction in a formal or informal setting.[9] While preaching may include teaching, teaching involves more explanation of the biblical text, and preaching involves proclamation.

From these basic definitions of the original words for preaching and teaching, it seems that both men and women can announce the good news and explain spiritual truth. As Yarnell and Yarnell explain, "The most common New Testament terms

---

[5] Strong's Greek #2097, "Preach," https://ref.ly/logosref/Greek Strongs, Logos.

[6] Gerhard Friedrich, "Κῆρυξ (ἱεροκῆρυξ), Κηρύσσω, Κήρυγμα, Προκηρύσσω," ed. Gerhard Kittel, Geoffrey W. Bromiley, and Gerhard Friedrich, *Theological Dictionary of the New Testament* (Grand Rapids: Eerdmans, 1964), 697, Logos.

[7] Gene Wilkes, "Discover Your Spiritual Gifts!" (Nashville: LifeWay Christian Resources, 2003), 1, https://youngadults.lifeway.com/wp-content/uploads/downloads/UnderstandingSpiritualGifts_List.pdf.

[8] James Strong, *A Concise Dictionary of the Words in the Greek Testament and the Hebrew Bible* (Bellingham, WA: Logos Bible Software, 2009), 23, Logos.

[9] William Arndt et al., *A Greek-English Lexicon of the New Testament and Other Early Christian Literature* (Chicago: University of Chicago, 2000), 241, Logos.

for proclamation—preaching, teaching, and evangelizing—do not generally restrict who may engage in such functions."[10] God gives the responsibility of fulfilling the Great Commission, evangelizing, and discipling to all Christians, both men and women.

The discussion about women concerns what *setting* we are referring to, the function of proclamation in the universal priesthood or the particular office held by a pastor/elder. Weekly exposition of God's Word speaking from the authority of the pastoral position is different from exercising the gift of speaking outside the office of the pastor, such as with itinerant ministry.[11] The difference lies in the authority of the office, which is what Paul seemed to indicate in 1 Tim 2:12.[12]

In discussing theologian James Leo Garrett's understanding of the universal priesthood, Yarnell and Yarnell deduce that

> the New Testament positively lays upon every Christian the responsibility of continual proclamation. No Christian is excluded from this call. The universal priesthood functions in such a way that liturgical proclamation must be continually practiced, whether in private worship or in public worship. Evangelistic proclamation to unbelievers also remains the responsibility of all believers.[13]

---

[10] Malcolm Yarnell and Karen Yarnell, "On the Universal and Particular Offices of Proclamation in Relation to Women as Teachers in Church and Seminary," *Journal for Baptist Theology & Ministry* 17, no. 1 (2020): 68.

[11] Jerry Vines and Jim Shaddix, *Power in the Pulpit: How to Prepare and Deliver Expository Sermons* (Chicago: Moody Press, 1999), 13.

[12] Lea and Griffin, *1, 2 Timothy, Titus*, 97 (see chap. 1, n. 14).

[13] Yarnell and Yarnell, "On the Universal and Particular Offices of Proclamation," 48.

Having attended many women's events over the years, I have observed various platform speakers. Some women proclaim truth revealing a speaking gift stemming from exhortation, which can be defined as emboldening another in belief or course of action, making a strong request or appeal.[14] Other speakers hold the teaching gift in which they explain Scripture well, while some women seem to have both gifts. Think about your pastor. Some pastors are more gifted in exhortation while others are exceptional teachers, and some pastors seem to exhibit both gifts throughout their sermons. When you hear someone say an individual has the gift of preaching, a more accurate statement would be the person has the gift of exhortation, prophecy, teaching, or evangelism. These gifts can be evident in a variety of different settings.

Whether God gives serving gifts or speaking gifts, women should use the spiritual gifts God gives them to carry out his mission. Important to remember is that Jesus calls all Christians to share the gospel and make disciples. Too many people around the world need to hear the name of Jesus for half of the church to hold back from using their spiritual gifts. Understanding what spiritual gifts God gives to believers and particularly what gifts he has given you is essential to stewarding those gifts.

Discerning Spiritual Gifts

I keenly remember the first time I taught anything about the Bible. I was in college, and my former youth minister asked if I would be willing to serve as a Disciple Now leader for one of his youth

---

[14] Arndt et al., *A Greek-English Lexicon of the New Testament*, 766.

minister friends. I decided to give it a try. Having never taught the Bible or led any kind of study on my own, I prepared and prepared and prepared. I was extremely nervous, wanting to make sure that I gave it my all. I studied the lesson, used different sources to help me understand the Scripture passages, planned games, and secured a few items for object lessons. I was as ready as I could have been. What I was not prepared for was the work the Holy Spirit would do in my heart throughout that weekend. As I taught God's Word, I felt my heart come alive. I could sense the Spirit working through me because even as much as I had prepared, the Spirit was bringing to my mind passages of Scripture to help explain the ones I did study. He was helping me recall how the Bible fits together as one continuous story of God. When I taught that weekend, I knew this was what I was created to do. The truth is I really kind of stumbled into learning about one of my spiritual gifts. That opportunity awakened something within me I did not know was there. Sometimes we learn what we were created to do simply by giving it a try.

Knowing what spiritual gifts you have been given is key to using your gifts. While sometimes we may already be operating in our gifts without formally acknowledging them as such, at other moments we may not realize we have a gift until it is pointed out to us. Operating in your gifts is difficult if you do not know you have them in the first place. Recognizing your spiritual gifts may be a process, but here are some steps you can take to identify your gifts.

First, you can *pray and ask the Lord to reveal the gifts he has given you*. Talk to him about how he plans to use you to serve his kingdom. Keep in mind that he has had a good plan for you since you were in the womb (Ps 139:13–14), and he is continually working out his good purpose in you (Eph 2:10). Second, *study*

Scripture for teachings on spiritual gifts. Check out the lists mentioned above and take the time to explore what the Bible has to say about spiritual gifts.

A third way to discover your gifts is to *seek counsel from spiritually mature people who see gifts in you.* Ask them to have a conversation with you about what gifts they recognize in your life. Sometimes other people can confirm what we already see or open our eyes to gifts we could not even see in ourselves. Next, you could *take a spiritual gifts test or consult resources about spiritual gifts.*[15] Check and see if your church has a process for helping people discover their gifts. Some churches participate with ministries that allow you to take a comprehensive spiritual gifts test. While not always a perfect indicator of gifts (mainly because of the human factor more so than the test itself), a spiritual gifts test can point you in the right direction toward discovering your gifts.

Finally, *try out different ministries to determine where your passion lies.* Ask yourself, "What is life-giving to me?" Sometimes you may not know the answer to that question until you try something. What motivates you to serve God? What do you enjoy doing? Friend, it is okay to enjoy serving the Lord! Ministry leadership requires plenty of sacrifices, but also it involves plenty of joyful moments. Serving in the place where God wants you brings with it a soul-stirring satisfaction that can be found nowhere else.

God has uniquely gifted you to serve in his church. So, begin to move in the direction of where he has called you by finding out

---

[15] To download a free spiritual gifts test, see Spiritual Gifts Survey at https://youngadults.lifeway.com/wp-content/uploads/downloads/Spiritual GiftsSurvey.pdf.

how he has gifted you to serve in the kingdom. Then start using your gifts for his glory!

Using Spiritual Gifts

God chooses what and to whom he wants to give spiritual gifts. As a woman, you have spiritual gifts, and God intends for you to use them. The church needs the spiritual gifts women have to offer. Without them, the church would be an incomplete body of believers (1 Cor 12:12–27). While church offices may be viewed differently according to your church tradition, spiritual gifts are not gender-specific. Where women often feel confused is when those opportunities are unclear. Again, churches providing clarity on where women can serve makes all the difference. Then churches can actively seek to provide opportunities for women to lead in those areas and highlight where women are serving. As women see other women using their gifts for ministry, they will recognize that God has a place for them to serve too. What opportunities for service look like may vary according to your denomination or church, but what is most crucial is that women find ways to use their spiritual gifts within the church.

Using your spiritual gifts does not require a title or a position. If God stirs your heart to give to others, give according to how he leads. If you enjoy organizing and coordinating people, find ways to lead to the best of your ability. If you like to encourage and inspire others, use your gift of exhortation to lift up fellow believers. If you thrive on explaining spiritual truth, look for opportunities in your setting to teach the Bible. If you have a passion to share the gospel, look for opportunities to have gospel conversations. These are just a brief sampling of the wide variety of ways you can use spiritual gifts with or without an official position.

God has a place for you to serve in his kingdom. You are gifted!

Questions to Ponder

1. What areas of service in ministry are life-giving to you?
2. What areas of ministry are not life-giving?
3. How can you use your gifts to build up the body of Christ?
4. How can you encourage other women to discover and develop their gifts for ministry?

PART TWO

Stewarding Influence Well

> Therefore, we are ambassadors for Christ, since
> God is making his appeal through us.
>
> —2 CORINTHIANS 5:20

Christian leadership encompasses stewardship of the influence God gives to his disciples. Jesus-followers represent Christ to the world and act on his behalf in their daily encounters with people. Stewarding influence well is a responsibility not to be taken lightly. If we want to live as ambassadors for Christ, we must consider how to represent him in a God-honoring way. In part 2, we will examine principles for leading from a healthy place with humility, confidence, integrity, professionalism, and practical wisdom.

4

Leading Yourself Holistically

"Come to me, all of you who are weary and burdened,
and I will give you rest. Take up my yoke and
learn from me, because I am lowly and humble in
heart, and you will find rest for your souls."

—MATTHEW 11:28–29

I have yet to meet a woman leader who doesn't describe her-self as busy. There is so much to do . . . so many people who need ministry. Sometimes we even wear our busyness as a badge of honor. Busyness has become such a common part of life that researchers have come to define the constant pres-sure of it as "hurry sickness." Hurry sicknesss is "a behavior pat-tern characterized by continual rushing and anxiousness; an overwhelming and continual sense of urgency."[1] I've been there. Have you? You know the place where you feel like you are constantly rushing and can't seem to stop even when you are supposed to be resting. When I did finally slow down for a season, I realized I had no idea just how hectic every day had become. Taking inventory of my life allowed me to refocus how I spend my time. One thing I learned is that I must prioritize my health. It's just not an option to ignore those things if we want to thrive in ministry for the long haul.

Leading others well begins with leading ourselves holistically. Typically though, when we are busy leading others, prioritizing our health comes last. Leading ourselves purposefully must be a priority to serve others from a healthy place. In ministry, it seems right and good to put others first because the Bible is full of passages that teach us to consider others to be more important than ourselves (Phil 2:3). We may even feel guilty about taking the time to prioritize our health. We think, *People need me!* Yet, Jesus set an example for us of prioritizing his mental, emotional, and spiritual health when he was here on earth (Mark 1:35). We also know Jesus would not have lived a sedentary lifestyle because, in the first century, people generally had to walk where they wanted to go. If Jesus needed to take care of himself, shouldn't we? Leading ourselves well means we prioritize managing our physical, mental, emotional, and spiritual health.

---

[1] Rosemary K. M. Sword and Philip Zimbardo, "Hurry Sickness: Is the quest to do all and be all costing us our health?" *Psychology Today*, February 9, 2013, https://www.psychologytoday.com/us/blog/the-time-cure/201302/hurry-sickness.

Leading from a Healthy Place

Physical Health

When I think about physical health, 1 Tim 4:8 comes to mind: "The training of the body has limited benefit, but godliness is beneficial in every way." Paul acknowledged two things here: physical training does have some benefit, and pursuing godliness is most important. As someone who went through a season where I was overly obsessed with exercise, I see Paul's point. Anything that takes our focus away from Jesus can quickly become an idol. In a workout-obsessed world, it's easy to do. Yet, physical health is not meant to be an idol. On the other extreme, when busy with ministry, I have also gone through seasons where I did not exercise. That was not helpful either. I'm now in a season where I am keenly aware that if I do not make time to stay active, my physical stamina for ministry will quickly diminish. So, let's look at a few practical ways to prioritize our physical health.

1) Pray for good physical health. I often prayed for God to bring healing when I was ill, but I had never thought to pray for good health until reading the book *Life Management for Busy Women*. Author Elizabeth George points out the importance of praying over every detail of your physical health, from wisdom on choosing health care providers to making healthy food choices.[2] I had quite an "aha" moment as I realized good physical health as part of the "everything" that should be included in my prayers (Phil 4:6). Praying for a healthy body is a great place to prioritize your physical health.

---

[2] Elizabeth George, *Life Management for Busy Women* (Eugene, OR: Harvest House, 2014), 56.

2) **Recognize health is holistic.** Your mental, emotional, and spiritual health affects your physical health. For example, some of the symptoms of anxiety include fatigue, muscle tension, sleep disturbance, increased heart rate, and gastrointestinal problems.[3] I can attest to experiencing all of those symptoms at various points when I have let anxiety intrude into my life. I tell my children often, "Your body will tell on you," meaning what's going on in your heart, mind, and soul will show up in physical problems. While our choices do not always determine our physical health (think Job), our mental, emotional, and spiritual health do matter when it comes to taking care of ourselves physically.

3) **Make healthy choices.** In seminary, I had a professor in a wellness class who used to say unhealthy choices should be the exception, but we often live in the exception. At our house, we try to avoid eating out as much as possible for both budget and health reasons, but some weeks our schedules get so crazy that we have a trash can full of take-out boxes. I understand. Making healthy choices is challenging when life is full of other responsibilities. I am not a health expert, but I know that I feel a lot better and get sick less often when I prioritize exercise and healthy eating. It's worth the effort. That said, I am going to stop writing and go work out!

4) **Maintain a reasonable schedule.** We hear a lot about balance, but maintaining balance is a bit challenging with the chaotic routine of ministry. A more useful concept for me has been the idea of rhythm. Rhythms have ups and downs but generally maintain a consistent beat. Some weeks my focus is more on ministry, and

---

[3] "Symptoms (Generalized Anxiety Disorder)," Anxiety and Depression Association of America, accessed August 29, 2022, https://adaa.org/under standing-anxiety/generalized-anxiety-disorder-gad/symptoms.

some weeks my focus is centered more on my family. Then for some weeks, I try to prioritize rest and renewal. Every week is different. Living with intentionality in each area of life allows us to establish a good rhythm of maintaining priorities amidst a busy ministry life.

Also, knowing your rhythm can help you be efficient with your time. Are you an early morning person or do you prefer late nights? What time of day are you most effective in your work? Author Carey Nieuwhof calls this the Green Zone. As the green light at a traffic stop, it's the three-to-five–hour span of time when you are at peak focus.[4] Understanding your rhythm can help you take advantage of the time when you feel most effective.

5) Get routine physical checkups: Many people no longer have a primary care physician in the era of telehealth and urgent care medicine. Yet, having a regular physician caring for your overall health is vital in the long term. And please, ladies, get your annual exams! Having two women in my immediate family experience breast cancer, both with early detection and doing well with proper treatments, has caused me to realize the necessity of getting regular checkups. Seeing the right doctors now could help you avoid preventable health problems later.

Mental Health

Caring for your mental health naturally helps you manage your physical, emotional, and spiritual health. Our thought lives direct our entire lives. Thankfully the Bible has much to say about our thoughts. My favorite passages include Phil 4:8; Rom 12:1–2;

---

[4] Carey Nieuwhof, *At Your Best: How to Get Time, Energy, & Priorities Working in Your Favor* (Colorado Springs: Waterbrook, 2021), 62–63.

2 Cor 10:3–5. In Phil 4:8, Paul encouraged us to think about things that are true, honorable, just, pure, lovely, commendable, morally excellent, and praiseworthy. Then in Romans 12, he urged us to renew our minds with the truth of the gospel. Finally, in 2 Corinthians, Paul admonished us to take captive thoughts that do not agree with the knowledge of God. All these verses speak to how we should manage our thoughts. They essentially show us two things:

1) **You can control what you do with your thoughts:** You can refuse to let negative thoughts have space in your brain. Author Sissy Goff calls this tactic "bossing" your thoughts.[5] I can relate to this because I am better at bossing than I want to admit! It reminds me that I get to decide what I allow to occupy my mind. We can either open the door to negative thoughts, or we can shut the door and keep them out completely.

2) **You can fill your mind with truth:** If we fill our minds with truth, negative thoughts have no room to take up space in our brains. Reading daily Scripture is not just something I do because I am expected to do so as a Christian leader; meditating on the Word of God is necessary for me to maintain good mental health. Even on our busiest days, we can take one verse and think about it throughout the day. If you continue to do that, building on each verse, before you know it, you will have learned a whole chapter.

I share these ideas with you not as a mental health expert but as one who has deeply struggled with managing my thought life. Too often, I have allowed fear, anxiety, insecurity, or worry not only to come in the door of my brain but to occupy every available space.

---

[5] Sissy Goff, *Raising Worry-Free Girls* (Bloomington, MN: Bethany House, 2019), 121.

I have learned through many struggles how to take captive negative thoughts and replace them with the Word of God. Almost twice as likely as men to have an anxiety disorder, women are adversely affected by the most common mental health issue in the United States.[6] So, you are not alone if you wrestle with managing your thought life.

Finding a counselor can be beneficial if you get to the place where you feel stuck and need an outside perspective to help you sort through your thoughts and feelings. A few years ago, I found myself in this place, and seeking Christian counseling was a beautiful gift to help me move forward in my Christian journey. Maybe you have experienced church hurt, or you are struggling to work through some issues in your family and need an outside viewpoint. *It is okay for ministry leaders to seek help!* There is no shame in seeking counseling when you need an objective perspective. As leaders, we often fear what others will think about us if they find out that we do not have it all together, but the truth is we are all in process. It is better to get help than to burn out.

Also, limiting social media intake has been immensely helpful in managing my thoughts. Social media can be used to create positive content and influence people for the gospel; however, social media can also tempt us to dwell on perceived lack. Being mindful of social media usage and its influence on my thought life has been a helpful strategy to winning the war of the mind. Experiencing the peace of God that comes through agreeing with the truth of God is worth the fight though.

---

[6] "Facts and Statistics" and "Women and Anxiety," Anxiety and Depression Association of America, accessed August 29, 2022, https://adaa.org/find-help-for/women/anxiety.

Emotional Health

Emotional and mental health are inextricably tied together. What we think affects our emotions, and what we feel affects what we think. Emotions tend to stem from the deepest places in our hearts, though, so sometimes we feel things and do not even know why. For example, have you ever said, in tears, "I don't know why I'm crying!" Indeed, hormones play a massive role in women, but we may also be dealing with some issues that we don't realize consciously in our brains.

The good news is God understands us even when we don't understand ourselves (Ps 139:1–2). Part of being made in God's image is our ability to feel and express emotion. As Dane Ortlund points out, "God is not a platonic ideal, immovably austere, beyond the reach of meaningful human engagement. God is free of all fallen emotion, but not all emotion (or feeling) whatsoever—where do our own emotions come from, we who are made in his image?"[7] So, the first step to managing your emotions is to talk to God about your feelings. Ask him to help you understand your emotions.

Next, you can begin paying attention to your emotions. Have you ever said, "I'm fine," and not meant it? We pretend to be okay when the truth is we are *not* okay. Essential to being emotionally healthy is being honest with ourselves and others. Write down what you are feeling. Then ask yourself why you are feeling this way and examine the source of your emotions. Sometimes that takes a little bit of digging. If you are like me, your emotions are like an

---

[7] Dane Ortlund, *Gentle and Lowly: The Heart of Christ for Sinners and Sufferers* (Wheaton, IL: Crossway, 2020), 73–74.

onion, and you must keep peeling back the layers to uncover the source. Then, you can consider different perspectives. If you feel hurt, misunderstood, excluded, rejected, or slighted in any way, try to look at it from the other person's perspective. They may not even realize you feel that way.

Finally, choose life-giving pursuits that will boost your emotional health. Indeed, not all responsibilities are life-giving. Ministry can be messy, and not all aspects of it are fun. The pandemic season even introduced the words "compassion fatigue" as a household term because we had become weary as a society of the overwhelming needs surrounding us. In those moments when ministry is hard and we feel like giving up, we need to ask ourselves whether anything we are doing brings joy and fulfillment. Reflect on why you began serving in ministry in the first place. What brought you joy then, and what can you incorporate into your schedule that will bring life-giving joy again?

Spiritual Health

Spiritual health is directly connected to physical, mental, and emotional health. If we struggle in one of those areas, our spiritual health will be affected and vice versa. Our minds, bodies, and emotions give us clues to what is going on in our hearts, but how often do we pay attention and make the connection? As Peter Scazzero observes, "God may be screaming at us through our physical body while we look for (and prefer) a more 'spiritual' signal."[8]

---

[8] Peter Scazzero, *Emotionally Healthy Spirituality: It's Impossible to Be Spiritually Mature While Remaining Emotionally Immature*, upd. ed. (Grand Rapids: HarperCollins, 2017), 46.

Being mindful of what's going on physically, mentally, and emotionally and then talking to God about it can help us grow immensely in our spiritual journeys. Authentic spiritual health begins with being honest with ourselves and God. Also beneficial to spiritual health is taking an inventory of your life. How are you growing as a disciple? In chapter 2, we discussed several ways to hear from God and grow in your relationship with him. In over twenty years of really pursuing Christ, I can tell you that consistent time in the Word has made all the difference. Yet, I have had to be careful that my time spent with Jesus doesn't become something to check off the list. Paul warns in 1 Cor 13:1 to avoid becoming a "noisy gong or a clanging cymbal" by growing in love. On more than one occasion, I have found myself clashing around noisily! So, in addition to growing in the Word, I ask myself these questions:

1) **Am I growing in love?** Jesus said people would know we are his disciples by the love we have for other believers (John 13:35).

2) **Am I growing in forgiveness?** As I submit myself to the Lord, he will give me the grace I need to forgive. Forgiveness is only possible by staying close to Jesus (Eph 4:32).

3) **Am I abiding in Christ?** When we recognize God is God and we are not, we can rest in him and follow his lead (John 15:5).

4) **Is the fruit of the Spirit evident in my life?** This is hard because the Lord does not always show us the fruit he produces through us, which is good. After all, we would likely become way too prideful if we saw all the ways he uses us. We can examine our lives, though, to determine whether any fruit is evident.

5) **Am I regularly engaging in spiritual disciplines?** Spiritual discipline lists abound and vary slightly according to the author

writing about them. The primary disciplines that I find most frequently listed are Bible study, prayer, meditation, solitude, fasting, service, and worship. We've already discussed the need for daily Bible study and prayer. Those need to be your priority, along with service and worship. God created us to be in a community to live among and serve others. He reminded us in Heb 10:24–25 of the need to meet together often. There is a reason why God designed us for connection. We need fellow believers to strengthen and encourage us while doing the same for them. Serving and worshipping together are two of the primary ways to stay connected to God and one another.

Meditation, solitude, and fasting are less often practiced disciplines but all beneficial no less to growing in Christ. In Christianity, meditation is not an emptying of the mind as is often taught in Eastern religions, but rather a filling of the mind with the truth of God. I think of meditation like a slow cooker, where you gradually let the truth simmer in your heart and mind. Richard Foster points out that meditation creates "the emotional and spiritual space which allows Christ to construct an inner sanctuary in the heart."[9] I love that imagery because in Ps 18:19, David wrote about how God brings us to a spacious place.

Solitude goes hand in hand with meditation as you create space for God to work in your life. Ortlund reflects that we should foster in our lives "unhurried quiet, where, among other disciplines, you consider the radiance of who he actually is."[10] I will confess that

---

[9] Richard Foster, *Celebration of Discipline: The Path to Spiritual Growth*, 3rd ed. (New York: HarperCollins, 1998), 20.

[10] Ortlund, *Gentle and Lowly*, 99.

solitude is the most challenging discipline to practice during busy seasons of ministry, but what benefits I have reaped when I have set aside blocks of time to be with the Lord. Ideally, practicing solitude involves setting aside several hours, a day, or a few days to be alone with the Lord. Like me, you may be thinking, *Who has that kind of time?* Sometimes I have had to force myself to make the time, but other times I have learned how to practice solitude in the few moments I have throughout the day. I have learned that I will miss out on what God wants to say to me if I fail to take the time to be still and listen for his voice.

Fasting is another means of seeking to hear God's voice. Multiple reasons exist for fasting, such as discerning direction, asking God to move in a situation, or seeking spiritual renewal. In the Bible, fasting involved refraining from food to focus on God.[11] Fasting opens our eyes to cravings in a way that causes us to turn our hunger toward God. Assuming we will fast, Jesus gave instructions in Matthew 6 on keeping a God-focus when fasting. Fasting should begin with prayer. Is God leading you to fast? If so, from what and how long will you fast? Jesus noted that fasting should be done with the right heart. Your purpose should not be to draw attention to yourself and exhibit false humility. Instead, your purpose should be only to seek God while fasting.

As leaders, we are busy. While service is important as a spiritual discipline, ministry activity is no substitute for your relationship with God. Prioritizing your spiritual, emotional, mental, and physical health is indispensable to ministry leadership. Fruitful ministry comes only from a fruitful relationship with Jesus.

---

[11] Foster, *Celebration of Discipline*, 48.

Questions to Ponder

1. How do you take care of your physical health? Make a list of how you are maintaining physical wellness.
2. In what ways do you manage your thought life?
3. When are you tempted to be dishonest with yourself and others about how you are doing? Take some time to journal each instance that comes to mind.
4. Where do spiritual disciplines fit in your life? How can you make time for meditation and solitude?

5

Leading with Humility

Humble yourselves, therefore, under the mighty hand of
God, so that he may exalt you at the proper time, casting
all your cares on him, because he cares about you.

—1 Peter 5:6–7

When my daughter was small, she decided she wanted to be
the center of attention one time when we had guests over. A
natural actress, she thought this would be her perfect opportunity
to show our guests her talent. She was dismayed to find out that our
company had come to visit with us, not just be entertained. When
I talked to her later about her need to perform, she shook her fists
and said, "I just want to be the QUEEN OF THE UNIVERSE!"
Silently, I laughed and thought, *You and every other woman on the
planet.* If we were being honest, she said what most of us feel. Don't
we all want to be the queen of the universe sometimes?

Pride gets us every time. It is the reason we all sin. Our selfish sin natures tell us that life is all about me. What I want is most important. The world should revolve around me. I should be the center of attention. Realizing the truth is painful. Life is not about me. I am not the center of the universe—God is. This is a lesson we learn over and over throughout our lives.

Surprisingly, there is freedom in knowing that life is not all about me. I mean really . . . what if the world truly was on our shoulders? We would be completely crushed under the weight. But instead, when we do feel crushed by the world, we are not because God holds us up (2 Cor 4:8). So, even though my selfish heart sometimes screams for attention, deep down I am relieved to know I am not the center of the universe. That's too big of a job for any one of us.

One definition of humility is "appropriate self-appraisal, seeing yourself as God sees you."[1] Humility is not degrading yourself or downplaying what God is doing in your life. In attempts to display humility, we can easily reveal false humility. I had a professor who said when someone gives you a compliment, just say thank you and move on. To do anything more than that brings the attention back to you.

Our culture encourages us to place ourselves at the center of the world and commands us to demand attention. Even in Christian culture, we are encouraged to build a platform and make a name for ourselves. In Genesis 11 a group of people tried to make a name for themselves too by attempting to build a tower to heaven, and it did not go so well. God did not allow them to succeed. God will not share his glory with another (Isa 45:5). If we are serving in

---

[1] Jeff Iorg, *The Character of Leadership: Nine Qualities That Define Great Leaders* (Nashville: B&H, 2007), 95.

the spotlight with any other motivation than to make Jesus's name known, God will humble us (Luke 14:11).

Serving with humility means we have a willing spirit to do whatever is required of the task at hand. If you are only ready to serve in the spotlight, then you have missed the point of Jesus's teaching that he came not to be served but to serve (Matt 20:28). As Jeff Iorg notes, "God highly values what happens outside the limelight."[2] Are you just as willing to clean a toilet as you are to teach a crowd? In college one summer, I wanted to serve as a camp counselor but instead was hired at the camp to cook. I chopped fruits and vegetables, served meals, cleaned tables and toilets, and did whatever else was needed. I learned valuable lessons about serving with a joyful heart, even if I would prefer never to slice a cantaloupe again!

Putting others before ourselves sets our hearts free to live the joyful, abundant life Jesus longs for us to experience (John 15:5). When we focus on serving others, our problems don't seem quite so big. The world's weight gets smaller as we rightfully realize we are not the center of the universe. We were never intended to be. So then, how can we serve with a spirit of humility? Showing respect for God and respect for those in authority over us is key to developing humble service.

> I have learned that . . . leadership is not about a
> platform or status. Leadership is about servanthood
> and putting your team—those you are shepherding—
> before yourself. The longer I am in a leadership

---

[2] Jeff Iorg, *Shadow Christians: Making an Impact When No One Knows Your Name* (Nashville: B&H, 2020), 52.

position in ministry, the more I am understanding that
leadership equates to putting others before myself.

—Taylor McQueen, Student Ministry
Associate, First Baptist Church, Opelika, AL

Respect God

Humbling ourselves before the Lord is the first step to respecting
God. Scripture is full of verses reminding us that God is God and
we are not.[3] I think my favorite has to be Ps 100:3, "Acknowledge
that the Lord is God. He made us, and we are his—his people,
the sheep of his pasture." I appreciate how the CSB version uses
the word "acknowledge." When we acknowledge something, we are
admitting something "to be real or true, recognizing the authority, validity, or claims of."[4] When you acknowledge that the Lord
is God, you admit God is real, God is true, and God has authority
over your life because he made you. We are his creation. He made
us, not the other way around.

Proverbs 1:7 teaches us that "the fear of the Lord is the beginning of knowledge; fools despise wisdom and discipline." Fearing
God means we recognize he has full authority over our lives, which
signifies he is in charge, not us. If I am belaboring the point here, it
is because as leaders we generally like to be in control. And leading
does require that we take charge because eventually, someone on

---

[3] Though not an exhaustive list, here are some great verses on the power
and majesty of God: Job 38–41; Pss 2:11; 8; 9:1–10; 19:1–6; 24:1–2;
29; 31:14–15; 33:1–15; 65–68; 77:11–20; 93; 95–100; 104–105; 113–
115; 145–150; Isa 40:12–41:29; 43–44; 55:8–10.

[4] Dictionary.com, s.v. "acknowledge," accessed July 19, 2022, https://
www.dictionary.com/browse/acknowledge.

the team needs to make a decision. To lead well, though, submitting ourselves to God must come first.

Fearing the Lord also indicates that we depend on him in every way. Andrew Murray observed that humility is living in "the place of entire dependence upon God," and pride is "the loss of humility."[5] Isaiah 66:2 teaches us that God is drawn to humility. He delights in our humble dependence upon him. He wants us to come to him with all our cares and concerns and acknowledge his work in our successes. The opposite is true when we are prideful. James 4:6 (NIV) exhorts us that "God opposes the proud." I don't know about you, but I would prefer to avoid having God oppose me. Rather, I want God to draw near to me as I draw near to him in total dependence (v. 8).

Pride is a sneaky temptation that our adversary uses against us. It can slip into our minds without us even knowing until eventually it takes over and destroys us if we are not careful. When you first begin leading in ministry, remaining humble is easy because you know you have no idea what you are doing. Once you get a little bit of experience, pride can easily creep in unnoticed. You begin to gain momentum, and you see God do amazing things. People begin to notice, and you may gain a large group of followers both in person and online. Before you know it, you go from "Look what God did" to "Look what we did" to "Look what *I* did." You may not admit it out loud because of course you don't want people thinking you're prideful. That's the problem with pride. The sin is not always blatant. Often only God and you know you are struggling with pride.

---

[5] Andrew Murray, *Humility: The Journey Toward Holiness* (Minneapolis: Bethany House, 2001), 16.

If you find yourself in that place where you are wrestling with pride—whether you are new to ministry or well experienced—talk to God about it. Tell him about your struggles. Be honest that your heart is willing, but your flesh is weak (Matt 26:41). If your heart is not willing now, ask him to change your heart toward him. The Bible is clear in Prov 11:2 that disgrace follows pride, but wisdom comes with humility. Not only does pride damage our relationship with God but also our witness of Christ to the world. Striving to build our own kingdoms through prideful behavior will ultimately hurt God's kingdom. Seeking God's wisdom by humbling ourselves before him is essential to respecting God and building his kingdom.

Respect Authority

Respecting authority naturally results from respecting God. When we have first submitted our lives to Christ, then we can submit to the authorities God places in our lives. Often when there is an authority issue with people, there is an authority issue with God. In thinking about respecting authority, I always come back to 1 Tim 2:1–2: "First of all, then, I urge that petitions, prayers, intercessions, and thanksgivings be made for everyone, for kings and all those who are in authority, so that we may lead a tranquil and quiet life in all godliness and dignity." This verse reminds us, first, to pray for leaders who have authority over us. Leadership is a tough job, and everyone who leads in ministry needs all the prayer they can get. They are likely making the best decisions they can, even when we disagree with them. Praying for leaders helps us remember they are human too and will soften our hearts toward giving them respect.

Next, we must humble ourselves and let those in authority over us do their job and lead. In other words, stay in your lane. Doing so is tough when you are a driven leader, but I have been in enough meetings where several people thought *they* were in charge to know that staying in your lane is best. In discussing second-chair leadership, Bonem and Patterson define subordination as "recognizing and accepting that you are not the lead leader."[6] Just as respecting God means recognizing we are not in charge of the universe, respecting human authority means recognizing when we are not the chief leaders.

God exhorts us to "submit to every human authority" (1 Pet 2:13). If you are serving in ministry leadership and have someone in authority over you, then God is calling you to respect that human authority. If you are struggling to show respect to leaders ahead of you, ask the Lord to help you submit yourself to their authority. The problem with respect may stem from pride in secretly wanting to be in charge, or it may result from unforgiveness if the leader has done or said something to hurt you. Talk to God about why you are fighting to respect authority. Ask for his help to respect those with whom you are serving.

That said, essential to note in this discussion on respecting authority is that God never calls us to submit to sinful behavior. If the leader in authority over you abuses that authority in any way, you should seek immediate help from the proper authorities.[7]

---

[6] Mike Bonem and Roger Patterson, *Leading from the Second Chair: Serving Your Church, Fulfilling Your Role, and Realizing Your Dreams* (Minneapolis: Fortress Press, 2020), 30.

[7] Ashley Allen and Melanie Ratcliffe, *Responding Well: A Guide for Women's Ministry Leaders to Help Survivors of Sexual Abuse* (PDF) (Ashley

Find out the process for your ministry setting, whether through an administrator, HR department, or committee that handles staff or volunteer concerns. If it involves illegal behavior, call the local authorities immediately. Seeking help is necessary when serving alongside someone who abuses God-given authority.

In addition to letting authorities lead, we can show respect through being teachable. Having a teachable spirit will go a long way in working well with others. Being a professor, I can quickly determine whether my students are teachable. Those who are not teachable tend to struggle once they begin serving in ministry. Teachability goes along with humility. Thinking that you know everything is rooted in pride. Being teachable means admitting you do not know everything and are willing to listen and learn.

Being teachable also means you are willing to learn from your mistakes. Failure is a part of life. When it happens, you take what you can learn from the experience and grow from it. Having a willingness to learn from your mistakes and asking advice from those more experienced are essential to working with a teachable spirit.

Finally, respect can be revealed through supporting the authorities God has placed over you. Encouraging those in charge, especially publicly to other coworkers or church members, can indicate that you endorse your leaders. Avoiding gossip and criticism are two of the best ways to support leaders. Negative words can spread like a contagious disease through an organization. Our words impact not only ourselves but also everyone who hears them. Galatians 5:15 warns, "If you bite and devour one another, watch out, or you will be consumed by one another." The passage is on loving your neighbor

---

Allen and Melanie Ratcliffe, 2019), 8, https://ncbaptist.org/wp-content /uploads/resources/Womens_Ministry_Sexual_Abuse_Resource-2.pdf.

as yourself through serving one another in love. By contrast, how often do we bite one another with our words? Rather than tearing down with our words, we can show respect by building others up through making encouraging comments about fellow leaders.

As a leader, people will follow your example. If you refuse to submit to authority or speak negatively about leaders, they will see that as acceptable behavior for a Christian leader. Likewise, if you submit to authority and speak uplifting words about your leaders, people will follow your example of humility. The way we treat other people truly matters!

As I mentioned before, our culture encourages us to demand attention. While speaking up for yourself can be right and good when necessary, doing so to build yourself up can be detrimental to the kingdom of God. Even in Christian culture, making a name for yourself can be tempting, but building God's kingdom is why we were created. Staying God-focused by respecting God and respecting God-given human authority is essential to leading with humility.

Questions to Ponder

1. In what ways do you show respect toward God?
2. In what ways do you show respect toward human authorities?
3. Are there any areas where you find difficulty with showing respect toward those in authority over you?
4. What challenges have you encountered to maintaining a humble posture while leading?

6

Leading with Confidence

For you are my hope, Lord God, my
confidence from my youth.

—Psalm 71:5

One day when discussing making new friends with my son, who was elementary-school-aged at the time, he told me he was good at making friends. Without hesitation, he said, "Yeah, it's one of my many talents." His words were so self-assured and matter-of-fact, aside from chuckling, it caused me to pause and think, *Do I exude that kind of confidence in all that I do?* As children we tend to exhibit bolder confidence than we do as we get older because we have had fewer life experiences to erode our sense of certainty.

As Christians, our understanding of confidence can be elusive because on the one hand, we want to exhibit bold certainty, but on the other hand, we do not want to be self-focused. To better understand what it means to lead with confidence, let's look at some basic definitions. Confidence can be understood in two ways: First as "full trust; belief in the powers, trustworthiness, or reliability of a person or thing" or second as "belief in oneself and one's powers or abilities; self-confidence; self-reliance; assurance."[1] Our culture celebrates self-confidence as a means of exalting oneself, yet for the Christian, confidence comes from full reliance upon God.

Depending on the Lord to be your confidence can be challenging if surrounding messages about your place and purpose in serving are confusing. For women serving in ministry, "imposter syndrome" is all too common, which is the feeling that you do not measure up and that others will eventually find out you are not competent.[2] I know I have experienced this at various moments. Leading with self-assurance means that we depend on the Lord for our competence. The enemy, Satan, desires for you to feel like an imposter so that you will hold back from using your spiritual gifts and being effective in God's kingdom. We must remember that God gives validity to our service, not others' recognition of our service. Leading with God-given confidence means you choose contentment in Christ, pursue godly ambition, and take bold action to minister to others in Jesus's name.

Contented Confidence

Depending on God for confidence begins with trusting the Lord to provide your needs, whether that be ministry opportunities,

---

[1] Dictionary.com, s.v. "confidence," accessed August 29, 2022, https://www.dictionary.com/browse/confidence.

[2] Stephen D. Brookfield, *The Skillful Teacher: On Technique, Trust, and Responsiveness in the Classroom* (San Francisco: Jossey-Bass, 2006), 76–79.

finances, or encouragement and support in serving. Having contented confidence in the Lord is a countercultural idea. In American culture we are encouraged to boldly look out for ourselves by obtaining all the possessions we can amass. Yet godly confidence comes from depending on the Lord to provide our needs. Over and over in Scripture, God exhorts us to place our confidence in him even when life is not going so well (Ps 112:7).

The apostle Paul wrote that he had learned to be content even when times were tough because God gave him strength (Phil 4:13). Often, we look to that passage for confidence-building when we need boldness to face the task at hand. Yet the context of this favored verse in Philippians is having the strength to confront life with contentment whether we experience lack or plenty. Experiencing contented confidence means placing our hope in God and trusting him for the outcome in every situation we encounter. We choose not to compare or compete with other leaders; rather, we focus on trusting God as we steward the ministry he gives us.

Avoiding the Comparison Trap

If you have struggled with learning contentment, as I have, you know that it takes strength to practice contentment. We live in a society that fosters discontentment, so practicing contentment can seem like an uphill battle. In a social media world, we are now inundated by everyone else's lives on any given day. We see what amazing things they are doing, what vacations they experience, or what witty things they can say. Thus, we feel the need to reveal our best moments online too. How many times have you altered a photo of yourself that you posted, even if it was just to change the filter to give yourself a more flattering light? Rarely do we post when we are having a bad hair day. Constantly comparing yourself to others will only lead to resentment because there will always be someone you think looks or has something better than you.

And for the context of this book, we compare ministry success. If we see other sisters in Christ having more social media followers, a larger platform, or larger numbers at their churches, the subtle comparison trap can easily sneak into our thinking. We may not openly say or even think we are comparing ourselves to others. Yet, where is the source of that discontentment? You begin thinking that God is not blessing the ministry you serve, the ministry context is hard, or the people are difficult. If only those things were different, then you would have success.

What is success in ministry though? Two words: *faithfulness* and *obedience*. We can sum up success in ministry with those two concepts. Are you being faithful and obedient to do what God has called you to do? That needs to be your one and only focus. It does not matter what anyone else is doing. Jesus reminded Peter of this in John 21:21–22. Peter wanted to know if John would experience hardship as Jesus had just predicted for Peter. Jesus kindly replied to Peter that what he had planned for others was none of Peter's concern. When I am tempted to compare myself to other fellow ministry leaders, the Lord often brings these words from verse 22 to mind: "What is that to you? As for you, follow me."

Avoiding Competition with Other Women Leaders

Along with avoiding comparison with other ministry leaders, we must avoid competition with fellow leaders. We are all on the same team! I learned this lesson early on, serving in ministry with my husband as he initiated partnerships with area churches. Rather than competing for students, we actively worked to partner with other churches to host events together. What we found is that it strengthened all our churches as we worked collectively.

Networking with other female ministry leaders in your area can provide friendship and opportunities to serve together. If you don't know where to get started, check your local or state denominational office. They typically have lists of churches and staff/volunteer leaders. If you are serving in a parachurch ministry, see what other regional leaders are serving in the same or a similar ministry as you. Also, there may be regional or national leadership networks for women that you could join. Conferences and seminary classes are great spaces for connecting with fellow leaders as well. Then regularly pray for women leading ministries like the one you lead, and reach out to make connections.

Godly Ambition

Godly ambition is the opposite of selfish ambition. Selfish ambition is something both Paul and James exhorted us to avoid. The word used in these passages, *eritheia,* conveys the idea of feeling resentful and jealous based on rivalry.[3] As discussed earlier, rivalry and jealousy have no place in ministry leadership. The word can also mean using unfair means to pursue political office for self-seeking

---

[3] Johannes P. Louw and Eugene Albert Nida, *Greek-English Lexicon of the New Testament: Based on Semantic Domains* (New York: United Bible Societies, 1996), 492, Logos.

purposes.[4] If we are not competing with others, we also need to ask if we are competing with ourselves. What drives you to lead? Is it to make your name known, or is it to make Jesus's name known? If you are leading for any other purpose than to make much of Jesus, I would urge you to check your motives.

Godly ambition does not include perfectionism, which is all about me and my need for everyone to think that I excel at everything I do. Often, I find that women in ministry leadership are ambitious people. If that describes you, then you are naturally going to be driven to achieve. Not only do you desire to achieve, but you want to excel with perfection. Then everyone will applaud and marvel at how amazing you are. We would never say that, but our actions might reveal otherwise. Going back to our discussion in chapter 5 on humility, the root of perfectionism is pride. God will humble you if you pursue excellence for any other reason than to do your best for Jesus. As a recovering perfectionist, I can testify that the Lord has humbled me on more than one occasion!

On the contrary, pursuing godly ambition means we are saying yes to the opportunities God places in front of us, even if they are not our dream ministry positions. What opportunities have you been given? Have you taken those opportunities, or have you held off, waiting for something better to come along, such as an official title or position to go along with your service? I have never waited for a title to serve. I just began serving and volunteering, and the positions found me. At times they were official, while in

    [4] Arndt et al., *A Greek-English Lexicon of the New Testament and Other Early Christian Literature*, 392 (see chap. 3, n. 9).

you may not even be about you. That individual may have a heart issue with the Lord. When receiving criticism, look for what you can learn. There's generally some truth to most criticism, even if the critique is embedded in harsh language. You can also consider the source. If the individual is a habitual critic of everyone, then you may not want to give a lot of weight to what is said.

Ask the Lord to guard your heart and commit Gal 1:10 to memory: "For am I now trying to persuade people, or God? Or am I striving to please people? If I were still trying to please people, I would not be a servant of Christ." Remember that you are walking in obedience to the Lord. Finally, pray for the individual criticizing you. Ask the Lord to bless that person. The person may still criticize you, but your heart will begin to change toward that individual. We must keep our focus on Christ and obey him no matter the cost to our popularity. Following Jesus requires taking bold action when called upon, knowing that our confidence comes from him.

Taking Initiative

Serving with bold action also means that we take initiative when necessary. If you see a need, you determine a plan to meet that need. The need might be something small that you can immediately address, or engaging the need might require developing a proposal to bring to your team. Taking initiative does not mean usurping authority of those you serve under. Rather, speaking up and making yourself available to accomplish needed ministry responsibilities is serving with confident action. If you tend to have a bold personality, you will need to pray for wisdom over when to move forward and when to wait for another moment. If you are reluctant to share your thoughts or take action, you may need to begin considering steps toward taking initiative.

You can volunteer to assume leadership of a new project or develop ideas for meeting a ministry need. If there is a task to be completed that you can work on without needing approval, avoid waiting to be told what to do. Just begin working! People notice if you are willing to serve without being asked, and those in leadership over you are typically grateful for it. Taking initiative to do tasks that are not assigned also shows that you are ready to take on more responsibilities.[8] Having a willing spirit that takes initiative to serve in any way needed reveals leadership with bold action.

Leading with confidence means you are content to lead in the space God has prepared for you. You are following God's lead, and your focus remains on him. You lead boldly, assertively, obediently, and resourcefully, depending on God to be your confidence.

Questions to Ponder

1. Where are you tempted to compare yourself with other ministry leaders?
2. In what ways can you network with other leaders?
3. How do you fight the temptation to pursue selfish ambition?
4. Where are you saying yes to opportunities God provides?
5. In what ways can you develop assertive communication?

---

[8] Becky Loyd, *MARKED* podcast, Lifeway Women, February 28, 2022, https://women.lifeway.com/2022/02/28/marked-becky-loyd/.

7

꧁ ꧂

Leading with Integrity

"But let your 'yes' mean 'yes,' and your 'no' mean 'no.'
Anything more than this is from the evil one."

—Matthew 5:37

When asking students what characterizes good leadership, authenticity ranks at the top of the list. In a world where prominent leaders (both inside and outside the church) sometimes struggle publicly, disillusionment can easily ensue when a favored leader experiences a misstep. For these reasons, among others, younger generations especially favor authentic leadership. They desire to follow leaders they know because they can observe the leader's life. They are not looking for perfect leaders, just transparent leaders who will point them to Jesus.[1] Ministry leaders can

---

[1] Mary Margaret West, *Show Her the Way* (Nashville: LifeWay Press, 2019), 16.

exhibit authentic integrity by living consistently, communicating honestly, and developing healthy boundaries.

Consistent Lifestyle

Leading with integrity means you are consistent and trustworthy in your speech and your actions. What you say matches how you live. Are you the same person publicly that you are privately to those who know you best? While none of us will ever be perfect, ideally, we are steadily moving toward Christlikeness. When we have inconsistencies, we must be humble enough to let people speak into our lives and point out our faults. Be sure you have someone, whether a family member, good friend, or fellow leader, whom you allow to speak hard truth into your life, letting you know when your speech and actions are inconsistent.

Treating all people as we would want to be treated is important to leading consistently. Do you treat everyone honestly and fairly, regardless of who they are, what they look like, or where they come from, or are you partial to those most similar to you? Recognizing where we may have implicit bias toward people who are like us will help us become more aware of our need to reach out to everyone made in the image of God.[2] Examining our dealings with others in all areas of our lives can help us see where we may need to make changes so we can be consistent in loving our neighbors as we would want them to love us.

---

[2] Natasha Sistrunk Robinson and Lilly Park, "Conversations on Race," in *Beautifully Distinct*, ed. Trillia Newbell (Charlotte, NC: The Good Book, 2020), 89.

Living a consistent lifestyle also means giving no one cause to question your integrity in your dealings with other people. Peter reminded Christians that we are called to be holy in all we do just as God is holy (1 Pet 1:15–16). We should be set apart because we follow Jesus. In 1 Cor 11:1, Paul boldly encouraged the Corinthian church to imitate him as he imitated Christ. Are you living a life that others could follow because you are following the patterns of Christ? Blaming those around us for our behavior is easy, yet at the end of the day, we are each responsible for our own choices.

Whether we have great examples to follow or not, we can all follow the patterns of Jesus's life. Do you try to be the kind of friend, daughter, spouse, mom, coworker, and so on, you would want to have? As we seek to imitate Christ, we must remember that others around us are emulating us as well. Paul summed up living consistently in Phil 1:27 when he said, "Just one thing: As citizens of heaven, live your life worthy of the gospel of Christ."

Living consistently includes being steadfast during challenges and crises, which we can only maintain through seeking the Lord for help. Leadership inevitably involves ups and downs. Crises will happen. You will have moments when you have no idea what to do, yet people are looking to you for how to respond. When life takes an unexpected turn, the first course of action any leader should take is to get on your knees before the Lord. Cry out to God for wisdom. If you are in a situation that requires immediate attention, pray silently while responding to the crisis at hand. Lead others to ask God for help. Often, crisis situations are new experiences for everyone involved. A prayer from Scripture that I repeat often is "We do not know what to do, but we look to you" (2 Chr 20:12). God will help you to be steadfast even when you feel that your emotions are all over the place. He will help you lead with calm assurance through difficult situations when you lean into his strength.

Honest Communication

Indispensable to leading with integrity is honest communication. Honest communication begins with being honest with yourself and God about what you really think and feel. Talk to the Lord about his plans for you. Then speaking the truth in love, you can let your yes be yes and your no be no. Often easier said than done, we tend to let fear of others' opinions keep us from honest communication. Referring to fear of people, Geri Scazzero notes, "If I say yes when I prefer to say no, I erode my integrity and hurt both of us."[3] Obeying the Lord may require us to say yes when we really want to say no, but doing so out of fear of other people damages our reliability.

Another way we fail to communicate honestly is when we say too much surrounding a no answer. If you feel led to say no, say it kindly and quickly. You do not have to offer a detailed explanation for why your answer is no. The more you say, the easier it is to lie about why you said no. Fewer words help you maintain your integrity.

In addition, maintaining honest communication necessitates choosing your words carefully. Just because something is true does not necessarily mean it needs to be said, and certainly if accuracy of facts is not verified, then it should not be shared. Are you able to keep a confidence? Proverbs 11:13 provides great wisdom here:

---

[3] Geri Scazzero, *The Emotionally Healthy Woman: Eight Things You Have to Quit to Change Your Life* (Grand Rapids: Zondervan, 2010), 128.

"A gossip goes around revealing a secret, but a trustworthy person keeps a confidence." Do people know they can trust you with information that does not need to be shared publicly? Ministry often requires confidentiality, yet serving in ministry does not give any of us the right to gossip.

Gossip only serves to tear people down and does nothing to build people up. If you are in a meeting, state your thoughts truthfully and kindly there instead of criticizing leaders after the fact. Even if the time is not an appropriate time to state your thoughts, you can avoid gossiping about the person later. Creating a team culture of honest communication will encourage everyone with whom you serve to speak truthfully and kindly in meetings while avoiding gossip afterward. Using divisive or slanderous communication spoken in secret is harmful, but practicing open, honest communication will build up the kingdom of God.

While speaking truth is important, communicating with integrity does not necessitate sharing every detail of your life. Living with authenticity means you admit to having weaknesses because you are human. No one needs to put you on a pedestal as if you were Wonder Woman. Yet authenticity does not mean you share everything to the detriment of those closest to you. Your story is yours to tell, while others' stories are theirs to tell. You can share general information about how God has worked in your life through situations without giving specific details. As you share, pray for wisdom about what to say and what not to say and obtain permission before sharing stories about someone else.

Additionally, communicating truthfully means you avoid using communication for ulterior motives. You avoid manipulative speech intended to get your way without concern for the other person's best interests.[4] Driven leaders can be tempted to think their approach is the best method and resort to using manipulative speech to get their way. When this occurs, achieving results becomes more important than the people involved. You may get what you want accomplished in the short run, but it will not endear people to you in the long run. What is your true motivation behind what you are communicating? Clear and honest communication concerning your intent will help you maintain integrity in your speech.

> People want leaders who are authentic and are not afraid to be real with them. They desire leaders who will come alongside them encouraging and supporting them in their walk with the Lord. They want leaders who invest time and love. It is important for me as a Girl's Ministry Leader to pour into all my girls with an equal amount of love, discipleship, and authenticity. I must be real with them for them to feel like they can be real with me. Authenticity is key in building relationships and trust.
> —Amanda Sweat, Girl's Ministry Director, First Baptist Church, Sevierville, TN

Healthy Boundaries

Maintaining healthy boundaries is necessary for upholding integrity in leadership. Boundaries look different for each person because we all have different personalities, temperaments, lifestyles, and capacities for responsibilities. Living with intentionality and knowing our own limits can help us live within appropriate boundaries.

---

[4] Bozeman, lecture notes (see chap. 6, n. 5).

One way to set healthy boundaries is to delegate. A temptation in leadership is to do for others what they can do for themselves. Over-functioning can be a result of fear and insecurity (*What if she does it better, and I am replaced?*), time constraints (*It's easier just to do it myself!*), or control (*I like being in control of everything!*). Yet we hurt others and ourselves when we fail to delegate tasks. Over-functioning can lead to resentment, immaturity in potential leaders, failure to see God's plan, and spiritual immaturity.[5] Delegating responsibilities can embolden other leaders and help us maintain a reasonable schedule.

Setting healthy boundaries with others can also help you to protect your personal time. You may have to put time with family or friends on your calendar as an appointment. If we are not intentional about carving out personal time, then life can easily become consumed with ministry responsibilities. For this reason, I personally do not have an email app on my phone because I know I would check it incessantly. Checking email on your phone is not wrong and may even be a necessity for your ministry. This is just a personal boundary that has been helpful to me. You do not have to respond to texts or DMs as soon as you receive them. Calls, unless they are urgent, can wait if you are taking a day off for personal time. Ministry can be a 24-7 lifestyle. You must be intentional to prioritize time for yourself and those closest to you.

That said, ministry also requires a lot of flexibility. Ministry is not a nine-to-five, clock-in clock-out kind of job. In the last few years, we have seen an even greater need for flexibility as life and ministry have made so many pivots. Boundaries will need to ebb

---

[5] Scazzero, *The Emotionally Healthy Woman*, 141, 147–54.

and flow and adjust accordingly. Being flexible means you are not rigid with your schedule but can set new rhythms when needed.

Another consideration for boundaries is that sometimes ministry attracts people who heavily rely on others to provide the emotional support they need. While they are learning to turn to God for support, they may develop an overreliance on people to provide their emotional needs. If you encounter someone in ministry who depends on you for more support than you can reasonably give, you may need to set clear boundaries, such as time parameters for texting or in-person conversations. You can let others know when you will and will not be available to text. You can also set limitations for conversations, such as by making appointments and clearly defining how much time you have available for a discussion.

At times you may need to set boundaries for how people speak to you. If you serve under someone who is consistently harsh and critical or find yourself with hurt feelings often after conversations, you may need to express how you feel when that individual speaks to you. You can use statements such as "When you say _____, I feel _____." Keep the focus on how you feel because of conversations with this person. This allows you to shift from blaming the other person to honestly communicating your feelings.

Often in communication we do not know how people receive our words unless they tell us. It could be that the others never intended to come across how you perceive them and expressing how it makes you feel will cause them to evaluate their speech. That would be the ideal scenario. The other option is that the person will refuse to make any changes. Even so, you will have communicated your feelings honestly rather than carry hidden resentment.

A final consideration to developing healthy boundaries is to respect the boundaries of others. If people need to set time limits on when they are available outside of time designated for ministry, then avoid contacting them during those times. Give them the space they need outside of agreed upon ministry expectations. Respecting others' boundaries will require that you plan ahead so you do not need to contact them during designated off times. If you desire for others to respect your boundaries, then you will need to respect theirs. Modeling healthy boundaries by giving permission for others to set boundaries will encourage those with whom you serve to lead with integrity as well. Practicing healthy boundaries will help you maintain consistent integrity and model for others what it means to demonstrate authentic leadership.

Living with consistency, communicating honestly, and developing healthy boundaries are essential to leading with integrity. In a world where authentic leadership is desperately needed, maintaining integrity is crucial to living a consistent gospel witness. When people know that you are real and that you can be trusted, they will be more likely to follow your leadership. As you live out the message you speak, you will lead with integrity.

Questions to Ponder

1. In what areas do you struggle the most to maintain consistency? What is one goal you can work toward to improve in this area?

2. In what ways might you experience implicit bias toward others?

3. Do you find difficulty in letting your "yes" be "yes" and your "no" be "no"? In what ways can you work toward clear, honest communication?

4. What boundaries do you need to set in ministry to guard your personal life?

8

Leading with Professionalism

Now as you excel in everything—in faith, speech,
knowledge, and in all diligence, and in your
love for us—excel also in this act of grace.

—2 Corinthians 8:7

When you think about the word "professionalism," you may
envision a corporate model of leadership. Yet what professionalism most commonly means is "the state or practice of
doing one's job with skill, competence, ethics, and courtesy."[1] Skill.
Competence. Ethics. Courtesy.

Shouldn't that characterize everything we do? As Christians
we should be known for serving to the best of our abilities. Leading
with professionalism is vital to maintaining leadership credibility.

---

[1] Dictionary.com, s.v. "professionalism," accessed June 17, 2022,
https://www.dictionary.com/browse/professionalism.

In 2 Cor 8:7 we can see Paul's masterful ability to encourage believers while also compelling them to keep growing. Paul pointed out that the Corinthian believers were excelling in their faith, speech, knowledge, diligence, and love. He urged them to incorporate that kind of excellence in their giving as well. Paul wanted to see believers grow toward full maturity in their faith (Eph 4:13–14). We all have areas in which we are doing well and areas where we need to grow. Pursuing excellence means we are working in that direction. This chapter is not intended to give you another reason to feel guilty about how you do not measure up. We are surrounded by those messages in the media daily. Instead, let's explore what competent leadership looks like as we grow toward maturity in Christ, exhibiting professional excellence, attitudes, online presence, appearance, and time management.

Professional Excellence

The characteristics of professionalism coincide well with Paul's examples of excellence. Let's examine them to determine best practices for serving with excellence.

1) Faith: Trusting Christ is the foundation for excellence, because our competence comes from God (2 Cor 3:5). This knowledge ends our need for perfectionism because we realize we are dependent on him and not on ourselves. Staying dependent on the Lord frees us to serve in his strength, not our own.

2) Speech: Being mindful of our speech is one way we treat others with courtesy. While the previous chapter discussed communication at length, I am reminded of James 1:26: "If anyone thinks he is religious without controlling his tongue, his religion is useless and he deceives himself."

I feel as if my toes get stepped on every time I read those verses. To imagine that my faith might be useless to share to the world if I cannot control my tongue makes me shudder. While there are many moments we should speak up, sometimes the most professional thing we can do is stay quiet. We can be harsh critics of one another. We can easily let envy, pettiness, or insecurity cause us to critique what fellow brothers and sisters are doing. Let's keep in mind that we are all on the same team, and we are all doing the best we can!

3) Knowledge: Growing in skill and competence requires that we continue engaging our minds. How are you motivating yourself to keep learning? Pursuing theological education, attending conferences, listening to podcasts, and reading widely are great options for excelling in knowledge. In addition to a stack of books on spiritual growth and ministry leadership that I generally keep, I have been challenging myself to read in other areas of history and literature. Being an accounting major in college, I looked a lot more at balance sheets than classic and historical works, but I am making up for it now. The statement "readers are leaders" is true. Those who desire to lead generally continue to challenge themselves toward growth in their fields. Consistently reading in various subject areas is a great way to expand your knowledge and keep growing.

4) Diligence: Working with diligence means we work quickly, earnestly, and carefully.[2] The word carries with it the idea of working hastily or not wasting time. Often in American culture we are encouraged to go to one extreme or the other. We either overwork with crazy obsession or go to the opposite end and spend our time

---

[2] James Strong, *A Concise Dictionary of the Words in the Greek Testament and the Hebrew Bible* (Bellingham, WA: Logos Bible Software, 2009), 1:66, Logos.

binge-watching our favorite streaming service. Working diligently for the Lord means we neither indulge in laziness nor let our work consume us. What it does mean is when we work, we give it all we've got for the glory of God. Are you known for being a hard worker? While working to please the Lord is our primary goal, working diligently will earn the respect of your fellow leaders and volunteers as well. When you work earnestly, people will know you can be counted upon to complete the task at hand in a timely manner.

Working diligently also means we don't quit easily. Quitting is the easiest thing to do when ministry gets difficult. The hardest thing to do is to keep going. Paul reminded us that when following Jesus gets hard, we have a great cloud of witnesses to cheer us on (Heb 12:1). On days when our work gets tough, we can look to Jesus to help us make it through. Some days our work is easier than others. Some days are just plain hard. Every day though, we can commit our work to the Lord and find encouragement in these words from Paul: "Let us not get tired of doing good, for we will reap at the proper time if we don't give up" (Gal 6:9).

While God often calls us to persevere through difficult seasons, sometimes he leads us to move on. Life is fluid, and we will not serve in the same positions forever. Whether stepping down to allow younger leaders to grow and flourish or recognizing you are at a crossroads in ministry, ask God for clear wisdom in timing. Sometimes roadblocks force us to consider whether God is leading us to make a change. If you are uncertain of what God is leading you to do, seek his guidance and continue serving faithfully until he reveals to you that it's time to transition to a new phase of ministry.

5) **Love:** Love is the guiding characteristic by which all believers should be known. When we love our neighbors as ourselves,

we will naturally be courteous. Your witness to the world is dependent on how you love fellow believers, whether in person or online (John 13:35). People observe what you do, and they will follow your example in how you love others.

Professional Attitude

Going along with loving others, our attitudes reveal the element of professionalism with which we serve. When seeking people to serve alongside me, I consider those who have a positive, eager attitude. Your attitude says a lot about you. Do you have a willing spirit to serve wherever you are needed? Do you figure out solutions to problems rather than build up complaints? Are you encouraging to others around you? We all have the occasional bad day where our attitudes are a struggle, but overall, serving with professionalism includes having a positive outlook. Serving others with joy is our privilege as ministry leaders. You are the front line to the gospel. Are you inviting people in or turning them away with your attitude?

Professional Online Presence

Online activity is a continuous reality in our lives. How, then, do we navigate our online presence in such a way that is God-glorifying? Your ministry may consist entirely or partially of online content creation. At the least, you likely use social media to advertise events in your ministry. In creating God-honoring content, first you must know your purpose for utilizing the online space. Why are you creating the content? Next, you will want to consider in what spaces you will employ the content. Each social media platform and website has a distinct focus. Finally, you will need to determine what you desire to communicate. If your focus is to honor Christ, you will need to evaluate everything you create considering that effort. How can you declare the beauty and majesty of Christ in everything that you post online?

Social media is a virtual public square in which many people seem to think Christian ethics do not apply. While they might say ethics should apply to all of life, their posts indicate otherwise. Essential to leading with professionalism is to consider what you post is just as important as what you say. Be mindful of any content that you create, share, or like on any social media platform. Before participating, ask yourself what this will reveal about your Christian faith. How would a potential employer perceive your online activity? Are you pointing others toward Jesus by what you say and do online, or are you pointing others away from Jesus?

How you respond to posts is just as important as how you create posts. When considering other points of view, keep in mind that speaking the truth in love is most important. Avoid sharing posts that are not factual, and give others the benefit of the doubt when responding. Try to understand from the other person's perspective before offering your own. Typically social media consists of sound bites or short explanations of a position. Having genuine dialogue about a subject is challenging online because you cannot fully explain what you mean by what you say in the same way that you can when speaking in person. It's important to keep that in mind as you try to understand the other person's position and respond accordingly. Also, you do not have to respond online to every social issue to validate that you have an opinion. Pray for wisdom over which issues to address, and speak up when God leads you to give voice to a particular topic. Remember that your focus must remain on being a witness of Christ's love, showing kindness and compassion in all that you say and do. Whether creating or responding to online content, let's look for ways we can draw attention to Jesus.

Professional Appearance

How we present ourselves is important because we represent Christ to the world. Having a heart to glorify Christ in everything, including our appearance, is essential to leading with professionalism. When you serve others, the focus should be on pointing others toward Christ, not yourself. You do not need to have a title or position in ministry to consider professional appearance. You do not even need to dress up if you serve in a more casual context, but you do need to remember that you represent the King of kings. Here are a few guidelines I use when considering my appearance:

1) **When in doubt, just change it out.** If you have doubts about whether something you are wearing is appropriate, changing into something different will eliminate the stress. If not, you will continually be self-conscious. Have you ever worn something and continually tugged on your clothing the whole time you were wearing it? The focus centers on you rather than who or what your focus should be on. Again, ask yourself whether you are bringing glory to you because you want people to notice you or bringing glory to God because you chose to look your best. Feeling confident in what you wear will help you think about yourself less and keep the focus on Christ.

Also, being mindful of your audience will help you choose appropriate attire. At times you may dress more or less formal, but considering your audience means you are respectful of different generations, genders, or cultures. If you are going on an overseas trip, you may be asked to wear something you would not ordinarily wear to a worship service. I have been asked more than once to wear a scarf during a service while in another country. Though I do not typically put on a head covering at my church in the US, wearing one did not bother me because I was showing respect to my hosts. Just be sensitive to your audience and remember that you are not the focus.

2) **Look your best. Don't worry about the rest.** Just as obsessing over your appearance keeps your focus on you, so does neglecting your appearance altogether. Giving glory to God in our appearance does not mean we disregard taking care of ourselves. If you appear unkempt, people will perceive you to have a negligent work ethic as well. Neglecting our appearance generally leads to feelings of low self-worth. The goal is thinking about ourselves less often rather than thinking less of ourselves.

In Phil 2:3–4, we are reminded that we should consider others more than we consider ourselves. Here we are not told that we should avoid considering ourselves. We do that automatically by default. Instead, we are told that we should strive to think about others as much or more than we think about ourselves. If we are too focused on our own appearance, then prioritizing others is a challenge. Ultimately the issue of professionalism in our appearance comes down to having a heart to please God. Do you desire to bring glory to him in all that you do? That's the most important question to ask yourself when looking in the mirror.

Professional Time Management

Managing our time well is a stewardship issue for ourselves and others. In Ps 90:12, Moses gave us a clue about how to make the most of our time when he said, "Teach us to number our days carefully so that we may develop wisdom in our hearts." Step one to managing your time, then, is to pray over your schedule. Ask God to give you wisdom in how to manage your day, what responsibilities to take on, and even how to handle interruptions in your day. Once you commit everything in your day to prayer, you will realize that God may have a different schedule for you than you do.

Prayer can also help us avoid taking on too much. We must be reasonable with the commitments we make. Sometimes we make commitments months in advance not knowing what life will look like at that point. More than once, I have made an advance commitment only to have other life responsibilities pile up at the time of the commitment. When I take on too much, I start to feel overwhelmed, and the tears start flowing. To avoid overcommitment, a helpful question to ask yourself is whether you have sufficient time to pray over the responsibility. If you do not have time even to pray for the opportunity, then you likely do not have enough time to prepare and participate in the endeavor.[3] We do not know what will happen when we take on commitments. Seeking the Lord is essential because he knows what he has in mind for us to do.

The second step to managing our time well is practicing self-discipline with our time. Some of us naturally tend to manage time well because our personalities lean toward organization. You may have an internal structure that lends toward discipline, or you may need external support.[4] If you struggle with time management, it may help to create a spreadsheet and write out how you spend your

---

[3] Kay Warren, *Sacred Privilege: Your Life and Ministry as a Pastor's Wife* (Grand Rapids: Baker, 2017), 91.

[4] John Townsend, *The Entitlement Cure: Finding Success in Doing Hard Things the Right Way* (Grand Rapids: Zondervan, 2015), 112.

time in a week, using hour increments. Put the things you want to accomplish on your calendar. Even if you are working toward a long-term goal, you can include time on your calendar each week to work on achieving that goal. You can also set reminders on your phone or use sticky notes. Ask a friend who enjoys keeping a structured schedule to help you create a plan. Find a system that works for you and keep working at it until it becomes a natural part of your life.

Regardless of personality, we all can be tempted to waste time. How many hours of mindless scrolling have you spent on social media? Before you know it, thirty minutes to an hour have vanished. All of us are lured toward laziness at some point by something. Seeking to honor God with our time does not mean we avoid any relaxation and rest, but it does mean we recognize our time on earth is short. The days we are given are precious, and we want to use them for the glory of God. Being disciplined with our time doesn't mean our lives have to be boring. As John Townsend explains, "Disciplined people don't have to be rigid, anal-retentive types, or authoritarian control freaks. . . . They really can be nice, relaxed, fun people. They just do the right things on a regular basis, over and over again—whether they feel like it or not. That's how they come out winners."[5] Good time management is the result of living with intentionality, stewarding the gift of time well.

A third step to managing our time well includes honoring others' time. First, we honor others' time by arriving on schedule for commitments. It means you can be counted on to be there early and stay until everything is complete for events. When you are leading a meeting, prepare ahead of time for the meeting so you do not

---

[5] Townsend, 110.

waste minutes trying to figure out what you need to discuss. Make a list of topics ahead of the meeting and send an agenda to those who will be included. Avoid chasing rabbits during the meeting. If the conversation gets off topic, you will need to steer the discussion back in the right direction. If you tend to get off topic during a meeting, then ask a fellow leader to help you keep the conversation moving forward on the topic. Begin and end the meeting on time. When people know you value their time, they will be more motivated to attend and participate.

Leading with professionalism means you are considerate of honoring God and others in all that you do. You recognize that perfection is unobtainable but that pursuing excellence is a worthy goal. You keep working toward leading with skill, competence, ethics, and courtesy in attitude, online presence, appearance, and time management, demonstrating excellence in all you do.

Questions to Ponder

1. In what areas can you improve your ministry skills by growing in knowledge?

2. How is your attitude toward what you do and the people with whom you serve?

3. In what ways do you exhibit professionalism in your appearance?

4. What is one goal you can set to improve in your time management?

9

Leading Others

Every wise woman builds her house, but a foolish
one tears it down with her own hands.

—PROVERBS 14:1

When leading others we can be known for one of two characteristics: being a builder or being a destroyer. Likely you
desire to be known for building others up, not tearing them down.
The problem is that all too often we allow personality differences,
conflict, sin, misunderstandings, micromanagement, and even lack
of preparation to damage relationship credibility that we have
worked so hard to develop. Leading others well means we learn
to navigate the complexities of serving alongside fellow leaders,
leading with vision, empowerment, support, and respect, as well as
through conflict.

Lead with Vision

Vision is a crucial component of leadership because people need direction and goals to have a sense of purpose. Vision is what drives and motivates people to move forward. The most important consideration for vision development is to pray and find out what direction God is leading for the ministry. Consult Scripture, as well as other godly leaders, and examine the circumstances around you, such as time, resources, and overall direction for the ministry. Remember that you are following God's lead first and foremost.

Next, developing a vision involves synthesizing ideas into one clear vision. You must have foresight to examine the potential consequences of the vision, whether good or bad. Then, you will need to develop a plan to implement so the vision can be fulfilled. Without a strategy to execute, the vision will be just an idea. People are more willing to participate in the vision if they have a well-organized plan.

Once you have synthesized ideas into a clear vision, the vision must be communicated. When communicating vision, take the audience into account. Reveal the vision as team members are ready to hear it. Then explain why the vision is important and how it fits with the mission of the ministry. An important caveat here is that your vision should fit within the overall vision of the ministry. Ministries should not operate as silos. If you oversee one area of the whole organization, then you will need to meet with those in leadership to convey the vision for your area and be sure that it adds to the complete vision of the ministry.

In communicating the vision, you want to give people a reason to support the new direction. Creating buy-in encourages leaders to promote the vision. Fostering support can be accomplished in several ways. First, clearly outline the benefits of your ideas to your leadership team. Then ask for their input. If people feel they have a voice, they will be more likely to rally around an initiative. Make provisions to involve as many people as possible to carry out the vision. When you and your team include people, they will support what they are participating in.

Lead with Empowerment

As you carry out the vision, you will need help. Delegation broadens the opportunities to develop additional leaders. If you feel that you are serving in a context where you truly have no one to assist you, begin to pray for God to bring additional laborers alongside you to serve. Then look around for God's answer to your prayers. Make a list of people you know. Pray about whom to ask. Then look for potential leaders who are spiritually mature, growing Christians. Believers who are faithful, available, and teachable are excellent candidates for leadership opportunities.[1]

Consider women who are unlike you. When building a team of leaders, be sure to include a varied demographic of ages, ethnicities, and life circumstances if possible. A benefit of building a diverse team is you get a variety of perspectives. Avoid assuming whether people will be interested in serving. You won't know unless you ask them. Then teach them how to fulfill plans for the ministry. Bring them alongside you and show them what you do. I like to call this "mentoring on the go." Leadership development takes extra work but is worth the effort.

---

[1] Kelly King, *Ministry to Women: The Essential Guide for Leading Women in the Local Church* (Nashville: LifeWay, 2018), 24.

When delegating, give clear guidance and then freedom to complete the task. Avoid micromanaging as it will frustrate your leaders. If you are a type A perfectionist, your leaders will thank you! Does everything need to be perfect? No. Does it have to be done exactly how you would do it? No. Keep in mind the bigger picture of the kingdom of God. While we want to serve with excellence, what matters most is that we are pointing people toward Jesus.

Giving clear expectations for serving can avoid confusion and frustration in ministry. Consider creating job descriptions for leadership opportunities. You can also create task lists or event forms that guide your team on each job that needs to be completed. Clearly communicating your expectations can help you get ahead of potential conflict. Ask those leading with you if they need clarity. Even though you may think you have clearly communicated, they may not have understood the information in the way you intended. Overcommunication is better than lack of communication.

Training is key to empowering leaders. As you develop leadership experience, forgetting that less experienced leaders do not know what you know about leading is easy to do. Guidance on how to fulfill the ministry responsibilities is a necessity for new leaders. Initial training should include information concerning ministry policies and procedures, job responsibilities, and expectations for serving.

Particularly important to serving is knowing how to handle critical situations. Ministry naturally lends toward counseling others, and training is indispensable to biblical counseling. While common life struggles may be addressed through lay counseling, more specific issues, such as trauma and abuse, will require a trained counselor. In her book, *Counseling Women*, Kristin Kellen notes that counseling is unique in that it often brings to light issues that require more training and knowledge than the average churchgoer has. Training in trauma and abuse is tremendously helpful before trying to lead a woman through the complexities of those experiences. More in depth knowledge about life struggles and the Bible's application to them are warranted. Many women need counselors who have been trained specifically in counseling as a whole or in particular life struggles.[2]

Often churches provide counseling through the church or refer people to local counseling practices. Leaders should be prepared to know when to refer someone to Christian clinical counseling, how to report abuse, how to handle crisis situations, etc.[3] Refer to the ministry you serve for procedures on addressing critical needs, especially counseling resources. As reporting laws vary by state, "a key element in understanding the policies of the church includes knowledge of the reporting laws for your state."[4] Staff members and volunteers should be well-versed in how to respond when situations arise that need to be reported or when individuals need a counseling referral.

---

[2] Kristin Kellen, *Counseling Women: Biblical Wisdom for Life's Battles* (Nashville: B&H Academic, 2022), 54–55.

[3] Some helpful resources on these topics include *Becoming a Church That Cares Well for the Abused*, edited by Brad Hambrick; *Counseling Women: Biblical Wisdom for Life's Battles* by Kristin Kellen; *Protect: A Youth Worker's Guide to Navigating Risk* by Jody Dean and Allen Jackson; *Responding Well: A Guide for Women's Ministry Leaders to Help Survivors of Sexual Abuse* by Ashley Allen and Melanie Ratcliffe; and *We Too: How the Church Can Respond Redemptively to the Sexual Abuse Crisis* by Mary DeMuth.

[4] Allen and Ratcliffe, *Responding Well*, 6 (see chap. 5, n. 7).

In addition to providing initial training, ongoing support can offer encouragement to keep going. You can give additional support through text messages, email, sharing podcasts or blogs, reading leadership or spiritual growth books together, or studying the Bible together. Find ways to show appreciation for the hard work and effort team members extend to the ministry. Let them know you value their contributions. Celebrate together all that God does in the ministry!

A final step to training is offering helpful feedback. When evaluating someone's performance, you may be called upon to give constructive criticism. First, you can pray about what to say. Start with positive information. Consider the other person's perspective and speak the truth in love. Listen well to her point of view. You will want to offer options for solutions, avoid generalizations, and be specific. Only hinting at problems may cause the situation to be worse, so using clear, direct communication when offering feedback is the most helpful. Finally, pray for the person as you finish your conversation.

A benefit of equipping other leaders includes expansion of the ministry. If you are serving alone, your capacity is limited. Bringing others alongside you can multiply your efforts. Another benefit is giving people the opportunity to use their gifts for God's glory. If we try to complete the work by ourselves, then we rob others of the joy of serving. Finally, others may be reached that you would not have been able to make a connection with by yourself. We all have different personalities, and we connect with some people better than others based on our personalities. Keeping in mind that it's all about Jesus can help you let go and let others thrive in ministry.

I learned over the years that when I have compassion,
build relationships, and take care of my servant leaders
(my church's term for "volunteer"), they are more willing to
serve alongside me. I want my servant leaders to use their
gifts for God's kingdom, whatever that may look like. I
do not place people in positions only to fill a vacancy, but
because that is where their gifts will best serve the Lord.

—Dr. Stephanie Cline, Director of
Children's Ministry, Winter Garden's First
Baptist Church, Winter Garden, FL

Lead with Support

In leadership you will need to build a support system both inside and outside of the ministry you serve. As you develop leaders to serve alongside you, you will be creating much-needed support and connections. Being friends with those you serve is healthy. The church should be a place of community. Avoid being too prideful to ask for help when you need it. While creating community within your ministry can be healthy and fruitful, you will need additional support outside of the ministry as well. Networking with like-minded leaders can be life-giving when situations arise that you cannot discuss with those in your ministry.

So, what about mentoring? A section on finding support would not be complete without this discussion. Often, I hear younger women express a desire to have a mentor. What they typically mean by that is they want someone to meet with over coffee for an hour or spend time with at her home weekly. Meeting regularly is a great way to develop a mentoring relationship, but let's consider that multiple avenues exist for mentoring. I have never had a long-standing mentoring relationship where I met with someone weekly, but I have been mentored in a variety of ways.

Mentoring can look like formal, regular meetings, or it can look informal, like learning alongside other leaders while you are serving. Mentoring can occur in small groups or in triad groups with one person meeting with two other people. Learning how to do something often comes through observing someone, asking questions, and then attempting it yourself. I have been mentored in ministry by watching fellow leaders serve. Then, I have asked lots of questions about why they do things a certain way and attempted it myself. I have also learned a lot through reading. Mentoring can occur through reading the works of other spiritually mature disciples. While in most cases I do not know the authors, I have grown a lot in my spiritual journey through their writings.

To seek mentoring, pray for God to bring people into your life who can guide you in whatever the Lord has called you to do. Then learn as much as you can from those around you. If you would like to develop a relationship with a more mature believer, take initiative to ask about spending time with that person. Start small by just getting to know a potential mentor. You do not have to ask that person right away if they would mentor you. Just begin to develop a relationship and see where the Lord leads.

If you have not experienced formal mentorship, you can still mentor others. I have mentored women both informally and formally. Be the mentor that you would want someone to be for you. Pray for God to show you women with whom you could invest your life. Then offer to spend time getting to know them. You can even bring them alongside you to join you in some of your daily activities. Whether formally or informally, we can receive and offer support through mentoring.

> The relationships I've developed while serving in ministry are simply life-sustaining. Seasons change, and some relationships are more significant in one season over others. Yet it's easy to see how God faithfully and lovingly provided each person, at just the right time, in my ministry tenure.... I keep a file of written support I've received over the years. While it may not be a big file, it's certainly the most meaningful. Proverbs 16:24 says, "Pleasant words are a honeycomb—sweet to the taste and health to the body." The times my senior pastor recognized my efforts, encouraged academic pursuits, or dropped a note on my desk to say, "well done" are important to me. Women in leadership may not always be understood or celebrated publicly, but meaningful support from those around us can encourage us to continue pursuing God's call on our life!
>
> —SARA ROBINSON, WOMEN'S MINISTRY
> CONSULTANT, KENTUCKY BAPTIST CONVENTION

Lead with Respect

One of Jesus's foundational teachings is the "Golden Rule": Treat others as you would want to be treated (Matt 7:12). This is a pre-school principle but one we need to keep learning over and over even into adulthood. With the Holy Spirit's help, we must intentionally be thoughtful to consider another person's point of view. Taking a moment to pause and reflect on how those around us are feeling can change how we react to others amidst the pressures of ministry.

If we desire respect from those we are serving alongside, then likewise we should show respect to them. We can show respect by listening well to others' opinions. I say listening well here because we can "listen," but are we really hearing what others have to say? Could you repeat back to the individual what was just said? Are you distracted on other devices, or are you giving that person your full facial attention? When listening to others, repeating their words back to them can be helpful to be sure that you understood what was said. You can say something like "I hear you say . . ." Summarizing a person's words can help her to feel heard and confirm that you understood her intent. With diverse perspectives also comes the potential for communication challenges because we have different backgrounds and viewpoints.[5] Be patient, listen, and try to understand the other's perspective. Thank team members for having the courage to share their opinions.

We can also show respect by showing care and concern for other people. If you are a task-oriented person, this is going to be more of a challenge for you. Get to know your team members. Take the time to find out what is going on in their lives. When a leader uses a commanding leadership style with constant criticism and little encouragement, people become deflated and lose motivation. Leaders who create a warm, positive emotional climate enhance motivation because people are more eager to work when they feel encouraged and know their leader cares about them.[6]

---

[5] Francesca Gino, *Carey Nieuwhof Leadership Podcast*, CNLP483, March 21, 2022, https://careynieuwhof.com/episode483/.

[6] Daniel Goleman, Richard Boyatzis, and Annie McKee, *Primal Leadership: Unleashing the Power of Emotional Intelligence* (Boston: Harvard Business Review, 2013), 14.

Finally, respecting others can be evident through our speech. Just as speech is important concerning those in authority over us, our speech toward those serving under us is crucial. Do your words build up or tear down those serving alongside you? Do you say encouraging words, or are your words laced with criticism and sarcasm? While constructive criticism focuses on the positive, consistent negative criticism will serve only to tear the other person down. The best way to test whether you are respecting others serving alongside you is to ask yourself, *What would those people say of me? Would they say that I am positive and encouraging? Would they characterize me as a good listener?* Giving respect through how we listen, show concern, and speak to fellow leaders is important to leading others well.

As one who tends to put tasks over people and strategy above relationships—a human-bulldozer, without Jesus—I've learned that the most stellar system means nothing if those we lead feel forgotten, run-over, or unappreciated. Instead of seeing every ministry roadblock as simply a problem that needs fixing, I must also consider the souls in need of guiding. . . . But if I primarily view people as problems to deal with and obstacles to overcome so that I can "build His kingdom," I've gravely missed the point of ministry. People are the ministry.

—Katie Orr, Bible Teacher, Author,
and Creator of Bible Study Hub

Lead through Conflict

Conflict is an unavoidable reality when working with people. We all have different personalities, different life experiences, and different thought patterns, which means that inevitably we will consider ministry from diverse viewpoints. Sometimes those different perspectives will align, and at other moments they will clash. Reasons for conflict may include differences in personality, communication, vision, theology, leadership style, or handling change.

Scripture reveals to us that conflict can happen. In Acts 15 we see that Paul and Barnabas experienced conflict and eventually decided to part ways because they could not come to an agreement over their issues. We also see in Matthew 18 that conflict can be managed. If someone sins against you, then you should go to that person to try and work it out. If the person will not listen to you, then you can take a couple of spiritually mature people with you to meet with that person. If that fails to solve the conflict, you can bring it before the church. Rather than gossiping about someone, we should always go to the person with whom we have a problem. We should try to work it out with that person directly rather than secretly criticize the individual.

Sometimes after all the attempts at reconciliation have been made, we may need to agree to disagree and discontinue the relationship. Paul and Barnabas did part ways for a season. Yet a positive result of them separating was that the gospel went forth to a greater number of people. The best resolution may be to move on. Reconciliation might occur later, or it might not. What we are responsible for is being sure we have made every attempt to speak the truth in love, handling everything with grace and kindness.

Paul told the Romans, "If possible, as far as it depends on you, live at peace with everyone" (12:18). Sometimes peace is possible, and at other times it is not. We must stand on truth. In negotiating peace, we never want to compromise our beliefs. Yet we must ask ourselves if this is an area where we can agree to disagree. Is this a matter of personal preference or of theological conviction? With theological conviction, establishing whether an issue is central to the gospel or a secondary or tertiary issue in which different viewpoints within an orthodox understanding of Christianity can coexist is necessary to determining whether you can continue working together. Knowing when to confront situations is challenging. If the disagreement is over preference, such as what should be the color scheme for decor at your next event, then the best course of action may be just to let it go. Picking your battles will save you much grief in the long run.

Conflict can be dissipated or enflamed. Some people create conflict for conflict's sake, and engaging with them may only make things worse. Factors that can heighten conflict include social media, gossip, antagonism, or avoidance. A great path to dispelling conflict is to take Paul's admonition in 1 Thess 4:11 seriously: "Seek to lead a quiet life, to mind your own business, and to work with your own hands, as we commanded you." Paul exhorted the Thessalonians to avoid doing anything that would discredit the gospel to non-believers. Social media thrives upon people not minding their own business. While much good information can be circulated, just as much inflammatory communication can be broadcasted. Keeping our negative opinions to ourselves can help conflict disseminate.

Leading others well takes vision, encouragement, support, respect, and wisdom. The investment you make in people will be the most time-consuming and challenging aspect of leadership, but the rewards you will reap for leading others well will have exponential kingdom returns. You will not likely see the impact of your investment here on earth, but God knows how you have faithfully guided people.

Questions to Ponder

1. What is your vision for the ministry you serve? Take a few moments to pray and write down the overall vision for your ministry.

2. How are you developing other leaders? Do you struggle with giving them opportunities to lead?

3. Who is your support network? Make a list of people with whom you network or would like to network.

4. What challenges have you experienced in managing conflict? What have you learned from those experiences?

10

Leading Practically

Whatever you do, do it from the heart, as something
done for the Lord and not for people.

—COLOSSIANS 3:23

In discussing practical considerations for stewarding leadership, remembering first and foremost that you are serving the Lord is paramount. You may have the opportunity to negotiate your needs and serve with supportive leaders, or you may not. You may develop rhythms for managing different seasons of life with ease, or you may not. At some point you will likely encounter various challenges in leadership, but as we seek to serve the Lord with all our hearts, we can trust God to take care of the things we need (Matt 6:33–34). In our final chapter, let's take a look at practical considerations for serving, working alongside brothers in Christ, and managing life.

Practical Considerations

Negotiating Title

While formal positions are not a requirement for serving in ministry, having a clear title communicates well to others what you do. When titles are unclear, people do not know to whom they should go with their ideas and concerns. Titles that do not match the job cause confusion about what responsibilities encompass the position. Titles also imply support for a position. If a ministry values a position enough to give a clear title, then people know that position is important to the organization.[1] Titles do not have to be limited to paid staff. A volunteer can hold a position with a clear title. Specifying a person's role helps everyone in the church or organization better understand the purpose of the position. What titles may be used for women in leadership will depend on the ministry's position on opportunities for women serving, but each ministry can determine the most appropriate way to express to the church or organization what the responsibilities encompass.

If you feel that having a more specific title is needed to communicate to others what position you serve, then talk to those in authority about making that change to create a title to match the ministry responsibilities. You may want to develop a proposal outlining what the job entails and the benefits to creating a title that matches the description.

Asking for clarity in titles can help navigate the best fit for the position you serve. When you ask, do so respectfully without demanding a certain title. If the outcome is not what you desire

---

[1] Cole, *Developing Female Leaders*, 124 (see chap. 1, n. 17).

because you feel as though you have been treated unfairly, begin to pray. Talk to the Lord about your need and let him work out what's best for you. While titles are not required for serving in leadership, they can be beneficial to clarify what responsibilities you hold.

> Something as simple as a title is such a big deal. Most people in my church still have no idea what my title is or how to express what I do. The previous male leader in this position with the same job description was Associate Pastor. I am the Minister of Family Discipleship and Administration. My pastor is the primary champion for me in ministry leadership. He invited me to transition from preschool and children's ministry to churchwide discipleship and administration. He challenged me to pursue higher theological education. He gives me opportunities to lead. He trusts my decisions.
>
> —Jennifer Foster, Minister of Family Discipleship and Administration, Heritage Baptist Church, Montgomery, AL

Negotiating Salary

I grew up around the car business. Negotiation was a natural part of life in my family, and I learned early on that asking for what you need is appropriate in negotiation. You will not know whether your requests can be granted if you do not ask. Before assuming a paid staff position, determine your realistic needs. If you have not established your monthly budget needs, create a spreadsheet outlining all your expenses in each month. There are fixed expenses (those that do not change, such as rent or a house payment) and variable expenses (those that do change, such as groceries). As I mentioned, be realistic. If you are going into ministry, living on a budget is a fact of life.

You do have to meet your monthly expenses though. Are you living beyond your means? If so, you may need to examine areas in which you can trim your budget. For example, one of my business professors in college showed us how much he was saving and investing by making his coffee at home while his fellow colleague commuting with him purchased a daily coffee. How much money he was saving and investing over time was astounding. I have been making coffee at home in the mornings ever since. While we all have legitimate expenses, there may be areas where you can adjust your budget. Once you determine your realistic needs, then you will know what salary you need to make ends meet.

You may also want to do research comparing salaries of similar positions at like-size ministries. The more data you can bring to support your request will show you have given serious consideration to your needs. While it may feel awkward to associate monetary value with ministry, Scripture teaches that a "worker is worthy of his wages" (Luke 10:7). If you are seeking a paid staff position, you can request compensation commensurate for the position.

Another consideration though is what the organization can provide. Budgets may dictate that the offer given is the most possible for the position. Ultimately what God is calling you to do is most important. If you feel led to serve in a position that cannot pay what you need, you will need to decide where God is leading. If God is directing your steps toward this ministry position, then he will meet your needs. Taking an additional part-time job outside of the ministry to make ends meet may be necessary.

If you have already taken a position, but the wages are not sufficient to meet your needs, you can outline a proposal explaining why an increase is justified. Perhaps you are serving in a part-time position that really requires full-time hours. If you feel that the position substantiates a full-time position, then you will need to give a clear rationalization for the change. Maintain records of the hours you work, including a detailed account of how you spend your time. Rather than giving a general request that may come across as a complaint, share comprehensive information on what the position actually entails.

Keep in mind if you accepted a paid staff position, you consented to work at the compensation level that you agreed upon. The organization may not be able or willing to pay you beyond what you've already accepted. In this case, Paul's admonition toward contentment in Philippians 4 is crucial. When discussing financial support of his ministry, Paul said, "I know how to make do with little, and I know how to make do with a lot. In any and all circumstances I have learned the secret of being content—whether well fed or hungry, whether in abundance or in need. I am able to do all things through him who strengthens me" (Phil 4:12–13). Paul learned how to practice contentment through all circumstances. Can you be content with your provisions?

Budget limitations may also mean the ministry cannot pay you at all and you serve in a volunteer position. Often in smaller churches, lack of additional staff positions available for women or men are a budget issue more than anything else. Sometimes taking a volunteer position will eventually lead to a paid staff position, though you must recognize that a future paid staff position is not a guarantee. Again, ask yourself where God is leading you and ultimately trust him to provide your needs.

Serving with Male Leadership

Growing up I admired my older brother and spent many weekends with him and my dad at the baseball field, watching my brother play while my dad coached. One day, when she was picking me up, to my mother's dismay, she saw me walking behind my brother and spitting on the concrete just as he was doing. My behavior was antithetical to the ladylike expectations of my cultural surroundings, but at around eight years old, I thought it would make me cool like him and his baseball buddies. Needless to say, I'm accustomed to being the only girl in the room.

The Bible teaches that men and women are brothers and sisters in Christ. This perspective should influence the way we interact with one another. One way of thinking about serving with men is to consider them "sacred siblings."[2] Because I have a brother, treating men with whom I serve as I would my own brother has come natural to me. If you do not have a brother or have not had positive experiences with men, working with men may feel a little more daunting. Developing this perspective and gaining confidence serving with brothers in Christ might take time.

In *Jesus & Gender*, authors Elyse M. Fitzpatrick and Eric Schumacher assert that serving together as brothers and sisters in Christ means "nothing more than recognizing and respecting, welcoming, humbling, pursuing, and devoting ourselves to one another for the glory of God."[3] They point out that the conversation regard-

---

[2] Sue Edwards, Kelley Matthews, and Henry J. Rogers, *Mixed Ministry: Working Together as Brothers and Sisters in an Oversexed Society* (Grand Rapids: Kregel Academic, 2008), 26.

[3] Elyse M. Fitzpatrick and Eric Schumacher, *Jesus & Gender: Living as Brothers and Sisters in Christ* (Bellingham, WA: Kirkdale, 2022), 102–3.

ing men and women in the church often centers on who gets to be in charge, but instead the focus should be on loving one another as ourselves. Men and women serving one another in humility is the way of Jesus.[4]

While humble mutuality in service is essential for brothers and sisters in Christ, working with men is often different than working with women because of the differences in how men and women lead. Though individuals may vary, women often lead from a more democratic, communal mindset, while men tend to lead from an authoritative perspective.[5] Because of the high value women place on relationships, they desire to garner more input from their teams. The relational emphasis women bring to leadership is a strength. When serving on a team with men though, they may or may not value input in the same way.

Women also tend to give much more detail in communication than men. When communicating with men, be direct and talk in bullet points. Writing out what you want to communicate ahead of a meeting can be helpful to summarizing the highlights of what you desire to communicate. You may need to organize your thoughts on paper to be clear and concise when it is your time to speak. I am generally a woman of fewer words than most, but even I can give far more detail than necessary when explaining my point. I know I have used too many words when the person to whom I am speaking looks overwhelmed. Everyone will be thankful if you do your best to stick to the main points.

---

[4] Fitzpatrick and Schumacher, *Jesus & Gender*, 105.
[5] Lee Gardner, "What Happens When Women Run Colleges?" *The Chronicle of Higher Education* 65, no. 36 (July 2019), A10, https://www .chronicle.com/article/what-happens-when-women-run-colleges/.

When determining what information to share, giving specific data can also be helpful. Providing evidence to support your ideas or proposals will show that you have done your research and given careful attention to your thoughts. Keep thorough records of any information that may be useful regarding ministry budgets, attendance, time requirements of responsibilities, etc. Being specific with the information you share rather than offering general observations will communicate more effectively.

Adapting one's communication to the style of the other gender to increase understanding is known by researchers as *genderflex*.[6] While you may adapt your communication style to work with men more effectively, you can also explain to men how you best communicate so they can more successfully work with you. If you need to brainstorm a bit and think out loud before concluding, you can clarify that this is the most effective way for you to organize your thoughts. If providing more detail would be helpful to the scope of the meeting, share that you need to include this information.

Adjusting your communication style to fit your audience may be helpful, but important to remember is that you should speak up! Your input is needed and valuable to the ministry. Avoid letting fear or insecurity keep you from sharing important ideas that would be helpful to your team. Use wisdom to know when to speak and when not to speak. There may be times when you feel led to keep your ideas to yourself for the moment. Ecclesiastes 3:7 reminds us there is "a time to be silent and a time to speak." Wisdom is learning to distinguish the appropriate timing between the two. Yet when

---

[6] Judith Tingley, "Genderflex: Adaptive Communication for Trainers," *Performance Improvement* 32, no. 4 (April 1993): 12, https://onlinelibrary .wiley.com/doi/abs/10.1002/pfi.4170320405.

God leads you to speak, remember that he has placed you there for a purpose, and your perspective is one that others may not possess.

Serving together as brothers and sisters in Christ also requires that we treat one another as such. Using wisdom in how you interact with one another is essential to maintaining integrity in ministry. If you view the men with whom you serve as your brothers, then it's easier to determine appropriate boundaries. Many ministries have policies on acceptable employee and volunteer leader interactions. Healthy boundaries can provide helpful guardrails for everyone involved in the ministry.

In efforts to maintain integrity though, the unintended consequences of some policies have been the exclusion of women. Unfortunately at times women have been viewed by what Jen Wilkin refers to as the three female ghosts that haunt the church: as usurpers trying to take authority, as temptresses attempting to influence men toward sin, or as children who are intellectually inferior to men.[7] These false assumptions can easily lead to excessively restrictive policies that do not allow women access to be a complete part of the team.

Sometimes policies are created as a reaction to something that has happened to enact the policy. Recognize that there may be history with the ministry of which you are unaware and policies have been put in place to avoid similar issues in the future. If there is a policy that you believe unfairly excludes you, then schedule a meeting with your supervisor to discuss the policy. Using specific examples, respectfully explain how the policy hinders your participation

---

[7] Jen Wilkin, "3 Female Ghosts That Haunt the Church," *Christianity Today*, February 12, 2015, https://www.thegospelcoalition.org/article/3-female-ghosts-that-haunt-the-church/.

in the team. Then offer an alternative solution that may allow you to more fully participate. While it may take extra effort to understand one another, men and women can have healthy working relationships as brothers and sisters in Christ.

Managing Life

Regardless of life circumstances, all women serving in ministry whom I have met describe themselves as busy. Ministry is not a nine-to-five job with a predictable schedule. Rather, ministry needs are frequently chaotic and unpredictable, which require an exceptional amount of flexibility. Often people do not see the responsibilities you fulfill outside of normally scheduled hours. Keeping track of hours spent can assist you in determining how to manage your schedule. If you are working on weekends or late into the evenings, you may need to schedule personal time during a weekday. If you need to explain to your supervisor the reason for adjusting your hours, providing detailed records of hours worked can give support to your request. Important to remember is that no one will manage your schedule for you. You must take responsibility for arranging your calendar, or everyone else's agenda will take priority.

Leading Single

A common assumption about singles is that they have more free time because they are single. Yet single women can be just as busy as married women. If you are single, you may have to address this fallacy frequently, but you can be kindly assertive in setting boundaries for how you spend your time. You need personal time for rest as much as anyone else. I was single when I began serving in ministry, and my supervisor told me to be sure that I took time for myself. He communicated that I needed to set healthy boundaries for ministry, and that advice has served me well.

Another concern for single Christians is that the church emphasizes being the family of God but often organizes ministry for nuclear family units. Serving as a single person can mean you are seen as a leader, but you are not included in family opportunities. If you are single, look for opportunities to build meaningful relationships with the families in your community and think of creative ways to invite them into your life.

On the other hand, if you are married, get to know single leaders at your church and invite them to sit with you at church or to have dinner with your family. If you have children at home, don't be afraid to invite singles into the crazy chaos of your family life. Include them in opportunities designated for families. Especially in transient communities where biological families may be far away, singles need spaces that feel like family. Often single leaders are overlooked because everyone thinks they are busy leading, but single leaders would love to be included in getting to know families as well.

The worst thing about being a single adult in the church is not being invited to do anything and hearing the couples/families all around you talking about the tennis they played together or the movie they went to see or the family game nights/playdates they had. This happens a lot. As a minister, people are constantly telling me how much they love me and what a blessing I am

to the church and what a great job I'm doing, and they
are likely sincere, but it often feels like lip service.
—Amy Young, Minister to Children and Families,
Stone Ridge Baptist Church, Alexander City, AL

If you are a single woman, you are valuable to the kingdom
of God. The Bible speaks clearly to the important nature of single
women's service to Christ. In a culture where a woman's identity
was based exclusively on marriage and motherhood, Paul said "the
unmarried woman or virgin is concerned about the things of the
Lord, so that she may be holy both in body and spirit" (1 Cor 7:34).
He did not say that single women should be focused on getting
married and having children to fulfill their purpose in life. He said
that they can be dedicated to the things of the Lord, and therefore
their purpose is to bring glory to God through devotion to Christ.
Your value does not lie in how much work you can accomplish
in ministry as a single Christian but in your identity as a child of
God. Your work is important to ministry, but your personhood as a
believer in Jesus Christ is most valuable to the Lord.

Leading with Marriage and Family

You can lead in ministry while serving your family. Having a spouse
and possibly children does not exclude you from leadership, but it
does require creativity to juggle responsibilities. You may need to
accept that sometimes life can be chaotic. When you feel that you
are doing well in one area, you may feel that the other area is suf-
fering. For example, while you are at a ministry event, you may be
concerned about what your children are doing. While you are with
your spouse and/or children, you may be thinking about all the

ministry responsibilities on your plate. Managing your time well can help, but being present and focused for every area of life can be challenging. Serving as a ministry leader, as well as a wife and mom, has compelled me to focus on the things that really matter and let go of the things that do not hold the same importance. As my children get older, I am keenly aware that you do not get time with them back. The time passes quickly, and the moments are precious.

Every family is different, so establishing the rhythm that works best for your family will be something you and your family will need to decide. Be careful to determine the difference between biblical roles for men and women and cultural stereotypes.[8] Does your understanding of household responsibilities come from what the Bible says, or is your perception of gender roles based on your family of origin or culture? For example, does it matter who loads the dishwasher or washes the clothes as long as the chores get done? Determining chore assignments at our house often depends upon our schedules each week.

Perceptions of household division of labor tend to be ingrained familial and cultural perspectives that we do not even realize we hold. Women often shoulder the bulk of household responsibilities, even when working outside the home, so it's important to ask for help when you need it.[9] Good communication with your spouse is crucial, and a shared calendar app is a necessity. With

---

[8] Sharon James, *God's Design for Women in an Age of Gender Confusion* (Darlington, UK: EP Books, 2019), 101.

[9] Amanda Barroso and Juliana Menasce Horowitz, "The Pandemic Has Highlighted Many Challenges for Mothers, but They Aren't Necessarily New," Pew Research Center, March 17, 2021, https://www.pewresearch.org/fact-tank/2021/03/17/the-pandemic-has-highlighted-many-challenges-for-mothers-but-they-arent-necessarily-new/.

busy schedules, especially including children, many pivots must be made throughout any given week. Intentional communication can help these adjustments to be made as smoothly as possible.

When appropriate, bring your children with you when you are leading a ministry responsibility. Let them see you in action doing ministry. Involve them as much as possible. I understand this is challenging when your children are very young, but as soon as they are old enough, let them see what it means to serve Jesus. Ministry can be a family endeavor, and your children will begin to see the reason you give your life to follow Christ.

If you desire to take additional leadership responsibilities in ministry but do not feel supported by your spouse, take your needs to the Lord. Talk to God about areas in which you long to use your gifts. If it is God's will for you to serve in this way, pray for God to open your husband's heart to that possibility. Kindly explain to your husband how you feel led to serve and how you plan to manage ministry and family responsibilities but be respectful of your spouse's position. Then trust God to work out his plans in your life. You will need support to manage everything well. Trust God's timing to lead you both in the direction of his plan.

Leading well in ministry requires careful thought to practical considerations. The more efficiently you can manage your personal needs, the more helpful you will be in serving others in ministry. As you grow in communicating your needs for practical concerns, serving alongside brothers in Christ, and managing life responsibilities, you will lead more effectively. Above all, seek the Lord and trust his wisdom to lead you well as you lead others.

Questions to Ponder

1. How could preparing a proposal support a request to meet your practical needs?

2. Do you find serving on a team with men to be intimidating? Why or why not?

3. In what ways can you more effectively communicate with male co-laborers?

4. In what areas can you work to juggle life and family responsibilities more effectively? How can you set appropriate boundaries for managing your schedule?

Conclusion

Stewarding the gift of ministry leadership is both a privilege and a responsibility. That God would choose to use us, mere humans, to communicate the truth of who he is to the world astounds me. Even more, that he would choose to use me speaks of the innumerable riches of his grace. What a privilege to minister to people in Jesus's name, and what a responsibility to lead well.

Before you finish this book and move on to the next one on your list, pause with me for a just moment and think about this:

God has chosen *you.*
God has called *you.*
God has gifted *you.*

Fill in your name in place of *you* and read those sentences again. Be reminded that God has a good purpose for your life. You are important to the kingdom of God.

God calls women to lead and serve in a variety of ways. Both men and women are indispensable to fulfilling the Great Commission. Yet for women, the journey to understanding how God desires for you to serve is often less conspicuous. The road may feel long and winding with barely enough visibility to see in front of you. That's okay. The journey of faith is not easily seen for all believers (2 Cor 5:7). Trust God to guide you on the next steps. I have been continually amazed at how God has faithfully guided me each step of the way. Though I would never have foreseen the road on which God has taken me, with each step of faith God has led me in the right direction.

Continue doing all you can to prepare yourself for what God may have planned for you in the future. Follow Jesus daily. Develop essential skills for ministry leadership. Lead in the places God gives you to serve. My prayer for you is that you would lead from a healthy place with humility, confidence, integrity, professionalism, and practical wisdom. May you steward the gift of ministry leadership well.

Afterword: A Word for Male Leaders

If you picked up this book, likely you desire to help women develop their leadership. We are grateful for men like you. Your attitude toward women serving will make the difference in whether women cultivate or stifle their gifts. While God ultimately opens doors for women serving in ministry, men often hold the keys to opportunities available to them. You have the ability to open and close doors of opportunity for women. Women who thrive in ministry often do so because of men who have recognized their giftings and given them spaces in which to nurture those gifts.[1]

I enjoy the opportunities in which I serve because of the men and women who have opened doors for me. Feeling supported by my husband, professors, ministry supervisors, and colleagues has encouraged me to continue cultivating the gifts the Lord has given me. Women, especially in conservative evangelical settings, generally want to avoid controversy, which is why they will hold back rather than overstep the line.[2] Women choose the churches they serve because their theological convictions align with those of their church and denomination. They just want an opportunity to use

---

[1] Cole, *Developing Female Leaders*, 78 (see chap. 1, n. 17).
[2] Cole, 18.

their spiritual gifts. As a male leader, you can help them discern where their leadership best fits your context.

Women need not be feared. They need you to celebrate and encourage the diverse gifts God has given them to benefit the body of Christ. Regarding perceptions of women and men, Fitzpatrick and Schumacher note:

> If men see women in the church as temptations, decep-
> tive usurpers, overly emotional liabilities to ministry and
> intellectual inferiors, true partnership will never occur. If
> women see men in the church as lords to obey, threats to
> avoid, or obstacles for advancing their own agendas, they
> will never be co-workers . . . believing men and women
> must view each other as both Jesus and Paul do. We are
> not enemies, threats, or competitors. We are siblings in
> Christ, allies in God's mission.[3]

Most women in the church are not seeking to grasp authority or influence men toward sin, and they are not intellectually weak. They simply want to serve Jesus.

Just as women should treat you like a brother, so should they be treated like sisters. Imagine how you treat your own sister or how you would regard a sister if you had one. While familial relationships often have challenges, generally siblings seek to protect one another. Ideally, siblings support one another and encourage the other to flourish. Siblings must learn how to communicate well with one another, especially brothers and sisters. If you have a sibling, you are likely familiar with the challenges of communication

---

[3] Fitzpatrick and Schumacher, *Jesus & Gender*, 76 (see chap. 10, n. 3).

and know that it takes work to understand one another. Seek to comprehend how you can serve well with your sisters in Christ.

Women generally make up a little over half of each local congregation. If we think about it using the analogy Paul gave of the body of Christ in 1 Corinthians 12, without the gifts of women, half the body would be cut off. For churches to grow and thrive, utilizing the spiritual gifts of women is essential to develop healthy, functioning churches. Women generally want to support their pastors. From the beginning of Christianity, women were some of the primary supporters of Jesus. Think about all the women who have supported you in various ways. Women in your churches are on your team. Find ways you can support them as well. Look for ways to include their input. Even if you don't have a staff position available for a woman, enlist women to offer insight on all aspects of ministry. Women are likely leading in various roles in your church whether they have a formal position or not. They have a lot of wisdom to offer based on their ministry experiences.

We are at a crucial moment in the history of the church where women need to hear your support and see it in action. Not only do women need to hear that you value their contributions to the kingdom of God, but they also need to see that you are willing to turn the key and open doors for them to serve. There are too many unbelievers in the world for half the body of Christ to be on the sidelines. Women need you to champion opportunities for them to get in the game and serve a lost and dying world that desperately needs to hear the name of Jesus. If you are already making spaces for women to serve, thank you. Please keep it up! Your voice matters in building up the whole body of Christ.

Scripture Index